MW01235357

GRAVITY SUCKS

MAGGIE ALDERSON

PENGUIN BOOKS

PENGUIN BOOKS

Published by the Penguin Group
Penguin Group (Australia)
250 Camberwell Road, Camberwell, Victoria 3124, Australia
(a division of Pearson Australia Group Pty Ltd)
Penguin Group (USA) Inc.
375 Hudson Street, New York, New York 10014, USA
Penguin Group (Canada)
90 Eglinton Avenue East, Suite 700, Toronto, Canada ON M4P 2Y3
(a division of Pearson Penguin Canada Inc.)
Penguin Books Ltd
80 Strand, London WC2R 0RL England
Penguin Ireland
25 St Stephen's Green, Dublin 2, Ireland
(a division of Penguin Books Ltd)
Penguin Books India Pvt Ltd
11 Community Centre, Panchsheel Park, New Delhi – 110 017, India
Penguin Group (NZ)
67 Apollo Drive, Rosedale, North Shore 0632, New Zealand
(a division of Pearson New Zealand Ltd)
Penguin Books (South Africa) (Pty) Ltd
24 Sturdee Avenue, Rosebank, Johannesburg 2196, South Africa

Penguin Books Ltd, Registered Offices: 80 Strand, London, WC2R 0RL, England

First published by Penguin Group (Australia), 2007

10 9 8 7 6 5 4 3 2 1

Cover design by Daniel New © Penguin Group (Australia)
Text design by Debra Billson © Penguin Group (Australia)
Author photograph by Adrian Peacock
Typeset in 13/17 pt Perpetua Regular by Post Pre-press Group, Brisbane, Queensland
Printed and bound in Australia by McPherson's Printing Group, Maryborough, Victoria

National Library of Australia
Cataloguing-in-Publication data:

Alderson, Maggie.
  Gravity sucks.

  1st ed.
  ISBN 9780143007050 (pbk.)

  1. Ageing – Humour. 2. Fashion – Humour. 3. Lifestyle – Humour. I. Title

penguin.com.au

Acknowledgements

This book would not have been possible without the following wonderful women. Judith Whelan. Cindy MacDonald. Deborah Cooke. Helen Long. Elaine Gowran. Roz Gatwood. Danielle Jackson. Catherine Clegg. Fenella Souter. Julie Gibbs. Jocelyn Hungerford. Fiona Inglis. Debra Billson. And two lovely men, Jim Hope and Daniel New.

All the pieces in this book originally appeared over the past few years, as my column in *Good Weekend* magazine. So if my daughter appears to go from a four-year-old back to a newborn, or fashion trends and seasons seem strangely out of whack, that's why.

For Julie Gibbs.

Contents

Fade to grey

It all started with a very bad haircut. I had to do something, because I had some kind of weird post-baby hair regrowth mutation, but the cut just made it worse. I ended up with triangular hair.

It looked seriously frumpy and no matter how many new products and styling tricks I tried on it – leave until just damp before blow-drying, blow-dry from wet with vicious strokes, scrunch dry, scrape back in Alice band, borrow wig from Joan Collins, etc – it stayed that way.

That hairdo had about as much style and allure as a bowl of cold tofu.

In the end it was making me so unhappy I went back for another cut, with a more senior stylist, at the same rug joint (my usual). It was a calculated risk. Losing more hair meant waiting even longer until I could grow it back into what I felt was my customary style – long, sleek layers with a hint of old slapper – but I couldn't carry on as Emma Thompson.

Natalie – the stylist – took one look at my hair and

sucked her teeth. She couldn't badmouth her colleague in front of me, but her face said it all: the cut was a total Barry Crocker.

She said it was a pity there wasn't a little more length to play with, but that we could sort it out by taking out some of the volume in the sides . . . Yes! Lose the isosceles – and cut out the disastrous razored layers, which bouffed up like a prize meringue no matter how hard I tried to plaster them down.

Razoring traumatises the whole hair shaft, apparently. Which is fine if you want to look like the lead singer from The Darkness, or one of his armpits, but not if Jennifer Aniston is more your hairdo role model.

'Oh, that explains it, then,' I said, greatly relieved. 'I haven't been able to do a thing with all those weird fly-away bits, and I've always had such obedient hair.'

And that was when Natalie launched her Scud missile. She pulled up a strand of wayward hair and rolled it between her elegant fingers, announcing: 'Oh, no, that's all the grey. It has a different texture. Grey hair is really wiry.'

Wiry. Now there's a word to conjure with in the thatch department. So my hair's not just going greyer than John Howard's pubes, it's the same texture too. I felt quite cast down.

I can still remember the day a hairdresser first told me I had grey hairs. The slow decay started round the back, so I hadn't noticed until she kindly pointed it out.

It was sixteen years ago, and the date is fixed in my

memory because that very morning there had been a blockage in the pipe between my flat and the mains sewer. My entire floor — beechwood parquet — had been covered in an inch of raw sewage. I had run away from that catastrophe to the sanctuary of my salon, only to be told I was going grey. I shed tears.

It's funny how the grey hair thing really gets to me, because other signs of ageing don't bother me at all. I've got perma-wrinkles round my eyes, a forehead like a saltwater croc, my breasts are sledging fast to the South Pole and the backs of my hands look like old treasure maps, and none of it bothers me. But the hair gets me down.

I suppose it's not the worst outcome. Surgery isn't necessary to hide it and I've got a whole battery of defences against the encroaching grey army. A very full head of highlights. Omega-3 fish oil tablets twice a day. Conditioner so rich you could pass it off as foie gras. Straightening irons. And best of all, Natalie, a brilliant cutter.

If only she was colourblind.

Downward dog

I just did a yoga class with Lara Croft. Normally I do them one-on-one with my teacher (worship worship, I am not worthy), or with my best pal, but when Caroline (oh esteemed yogi master) rang and asked did I mind doing a class with X?, I said 'Fine', expecting another gently fading peri-menopausal gal.

Then, as I entered the 'shala' (yoga language for 'school' – I'm getting quite fluent in Sanskrit), Caroline casually said, 'X is great. You'll love her. She's a fight chore-ographer for films.'

Forget downward-facing dog (a key yoga pose), I was downward-facing-hearted. And all my worst fears were realised when a piece of elastic walked in wearing a very fit-ted leotard and a Tom Cruise smile. Hello X.

Furthering the seepage of my self-esteem through the soles of my feet – be they planted ever so firmly, with big toes touching and heels apart, other toes perfectly asplay – I got the mat in front of the 'suicide mirror', an evil object which adds twenty kilos to your weight and about ten years to your age.

X was very nice about changing places with me.

She then told Goddess Guru Caroline that she was a little concerned about a slight injury she had in one hand. 'How did you do it?' I enquired, determined to be nice.

'Doing handstands in my kitchen,' X replied, grinning winningly. She was a great girl. I hated her guts.

Oh, I tried just to enjoy my class. I concentrated on my *pranayama*, the power of the breath, meditating on the exhalation like the sound of the sea in the back of the nose, or is it the throat? Whatever.

Anyway, while marvelling at the amazing power of the out-breath to enable me to get my head just a little closer to the floor with my legs akimbo, I couldn't help noticing that X had her entire upper body flat against it and was doing a crossword. Well, not really, but that's how relaxed she looked.

And, even while I gazed into infinity, as directed by Mr Iyengar, the disloyal corners of my eyes kept telling me that X was jumping between postures, as lightly as a flea, while I lumbered like a mud-stuck hippo. Also that she was totally doing the splits, while I was doing something more approaching the hokey-pokey, as I fumbled around for blocks to support my buckling limbs before collapsing backwards in a giggling heap.

And I did giggle. I snickered right through that class. Goddess Caroline calls all the postures – the *asanas* – by their correct Sanskrit names, you see, so that 'standing for-ward bend' is *Uttanasana*, 'plank' is *Chaturanga Dandasana* and 'supine twist' is *Supta Matsyendrasana*.

Except I have my own names for them. Bad-ass-ana. Fat-ass-ana. Shift-yo-ass-ana. I know it's childish, but those last syllables just cry out for it. I managed to keep these little gems to myself (along with my personal favourite, 'been-downward-facing-dog-so-long-it-feels-like-up-to-me-asana'), until I fell in a heap on the floor a second time while trying to attempt something half upside-down with one leg in the air, and loudly declared I was featuring a new pose called 'Maggie-asana'.

Caroline was very nice about it. I think she understood at some deep karmic level that being the naughty girl in class was the only thing keeping me going with Lara Croft at my side. Which was jolly decent of her, considering that the whole point of yoga is that – unlike ghastly aerobics classes – it's not supposed to be competitive. It's a private inner journey, not an exterior expression of ego. It will never be an Olympic event. If you're doing yoga properly you shouldn't even be aware of anyone else in the class. You should be present entirely in the moment, in a state of one-ness with the universe, wholly inhabiting your breath and your body.

Not wasting vital *prana* (life force) thinking how much you would rather be inhabiting the body on the mat next to you.

Bikini Babylon

'Bikinis after forty – good or bad idea?' This was a recent coverline on one of my favourite weekly sleb trivia trash mags and I turned immediately to check it out. It's a subject that's been on my mind for a while and I wanted to see what they had to say about it. There were pictures of Elle, Madonna and Sadie (Frost – Jude's ex) who are all over forty, all multiple mums, and all cavorting happily in bikinis. Elle was *running* in hers, but then, she would, wouldn't she? If I had her body, I'd never wear anything but a bikini. A string.

They all looked great and the magazine decreed that if you looked as good as they did – with fitness regimes which basically are their jobs, as opposed to needing to be fitted in around real life, like the rest of us – it was fine to wear a bikini. But real-life, normal, pudgy over-forty gals? No way.

Then I read something else on the subject, in an interview with Liz Hurley, the owner of the body beautiful which inhabited That Versace Dress, and who has recently launched a swimwear label – and modelled for her own publicity wearing it. 'I'm never again going to sit eating lunch on a boat in just a skimpy bikini,' she said. 'I don't feel comfortable doing that any more. I know that sounds bizarre coming from a woman who's photographed half-naked in bikinis, but I feel self-conscious posing for those pictures, and they're all retouched anyway.' I was gobsmacked. Impressed by her honesty about the retouching, but really astonished that she feels self-conscious in a bikini. The thing is, you see, at well over forty, I've recently started wearing them again.

The last time I wore one because I meant it was over fifteen years ago. Since then, I've been surfside in a series of dispiriting one-pieces. Apart from one in snakeskin print, which laced up the front rather saucily, I never felt remotely excited about putting them on. They were just something to wear to avoid arrest while swimming in public places. They did the job and that was it.

The move back towards the two-piece began with the marvellous tankini. What a brilliant invention. Tummy covered to walk about, but if you want to shine some rays on it (through sunblock, of course), you can just pull it up – after you have lain down flat. Brilliant. I even made my own. I bought a great leopard-print bikini bottom and then wore it with a plain black T-shirt bra, with a lightweight black singlet over the top.

After a couple of summers in that rig-out, without really thinking about it, I started taking the singlet fully off to sunbake (in the shade), and then one day I found myself in the ocean without it on. My tummy hadn't felt the caress of sea water for years and it was wonderful.

So it was a relatively short step from that to buying an actual bikini again. And then another. And another. And mixing them up, like Kate Moss, except with saggy bosoms and flabby thighs. But the thing is, I don't care any more. I'm over forty, I'm a mum, I've got a mummy tummy and I don't give a damn.

There is nothing more gorgeous than feeling the air, the sun and the sea on your skin and I don't see why I should miss out on that just because I don't confirm to our society's ideal of beauty, ie Elle McP.

So if anyone finds the sight of me repulsive in my weird bikini combos (it's not just copying Kate – I've yet to find one that fits properly in both the top and the bottom), I have one piece of advice for them: get darker sunnies.

Fourteen

The age of fourteen should be stopped. It should be officially banned. It's so unfair – on the young personages themselves and also on their parents, who have to go through a period of grief that their darling young Henry or Henrietta has been taken from them. In his/her place is suddenly a gawky weirdo whose limbs have been put on all wrong and who can't speak in intelligible sentences. And they have spots.

I do remember being fourteen so clearly myself. My body had declared unilateral independence and was sprouting pseudopodia in all kinds of unlikely places, apparently overnight. I was growing bosoms at an alarming rate, but the rest of me didn't change to match, except I was suddenly covered in a thick layer of blubber that was like wearing a diving suit all the time. I felt like such a galumpher.

I can remember so clearly my favoured outfit of that very hot summer. I wore an ankle-length Laura Ashley skirt, with some kind of weird shirt and then a green button-through smock over the top. The smock was 100 per cent man-made fibre and really nasty in every regard, but I wore it every day because it had exactly the right effect — it hid my entire body. And the spots on my back.

Up until that point I had been quite a normal, healthy child. I was an unbelievably fat baby, but once the overfed infant of parents who had lived through war-time rationing matured enough to run and jump and generally shake off the excess adipose, I was a svelte little thing.

I have pictures of myself, aged about eight, jumping in and out of a swimming pool like a shiny brown seal, everything in the right place. Then suddenly I was rendered a blob. Just as suddenly a couple of years later, it all shape-shifted again and I was a bit of a slinky teenage dirtbag babe. It was just those years in the middle that were terrifying.

Over the last few years I have watched my sister's two daughters go through exactly the same process. Even their faces went all weird. It was quite alarming. Now both have emerged into their gorgeous swan states and are just as pretty as their childhood potential hinted they would be. It's such a relief.

What I have only just realised is that the terrible fourteen effect is just as bad for boys. My beloved oldest nephew is now at that awful age. Gone is the dear little fellow who used to send me his home-drawn cartoon strips, and in his place is this alien being. With a permanent cold. And an attitude.

It could be worse — he has a really cool spiky insect hairdo, a prototype six-pack from the endless hours he spends perfecting spins, wheelies, jumps and turns on his bicycle (his fifth limb), and a CD collection that includes the complete works of Korn and Slipknot, but he's still a tweenie geek.

His voice has finally broken properly – he's over the cracked violin stage – but still he's unable to communicate in anything more sophisticated than grunts and sniggers. Trying to have a conversation with him is like listening to Beavis and Butthead on a loop tape. I still love him madly, but it will be a relief when he re-emerges in about three years as a grown-up version of the adorable little man he was at ten.

All I can say to fourteen-year-olds – and their bewildered parents – is that it will change. Think of this as the chrysalis stage of their development, from which they will emerge as beautiful butterflies.

If only we could spend those years in an actual chrysalis, it would be so much easier for everybody.

Ageing disgracefully

I was sitting in the hairdresser the other day when I became fixated on the woman next to me. What first attracted my attention were her toenails: resplendent in paper pedicure slippers, they were painted a gleaming metallic peacock-blue.

While attempting to maintain a level of discretion, I looked up to where the manicurist was still at work and saw she was having the same colour applied to her fingernails. That in itself was not particularly amazing – I remember wearing that zippy shade myself in the mid-1990s – but it was a little more surprising on a woman of seventy-plus.

Especially with the rest of her look.

Beneath the hairdressing cape I could see only her pants – and that was enough. They were zebra print with a bold tropical flower overpattern. Not what you could call subtle; in fact, they were probably Roberto Cavalli.

The hair the stylist was at work on – with very large rollers and ozone layer-threatening amounts of spray – was bright white Debbie Harry blonde. Verticality seemed to be what they were aiming for. Her skin, in contrast to the barnet, was a quite bright orange; she hadn't stinted with the make-up trowel and she was wearing plenty of bullion on both alligator-skin hands.

I confess my first reaction was: Eek! What is it? Someone get the bug spray!

My next thought was: Aha! She must be someone famously colourful to get about like that. Phyllis Diller perhaps, or Zandra Rhodes, but a quick neck jerk, as if glancing casually at the salon door, effected a good look at her head and it wasn't one I knew. She was just a ghastly, garish old trout.

But then, as I continued to check her out while pretending to read my paper, at some risk of developing a permanent strabismus, I had a revelation. She wasn't trouty at all. She was fabulous. And what a nasty little prejudice that was to sit with (although more comfortable than trying to look sideways without moving one's head).

I couldn't believe I had entertained it even for a moment – the notion that older women 'shouldn't' wear bright blue toenail polish, tropical pants, violently coral lipstick and vertical bombshell hair. Did I mention the toe ring?

What utter nonsense that imposed stricture of 'age-appropriate' appearance is, because even from my slitty-eyed, surreptitious viewpoint, it was quite clear that far from being some tragic, superannuated bimbo, Mrs Peacock had discovered the joy of growing old disgracefully. She wasn't inappropriate, she was just fantastically confident. In fact, she was the living embodiment of the philosophy outlined by Jenny Joseph in her wonderful poem 'Warning (When I Am an Old Woman I Shall Wear Purple)'. I wish I could just print it all here – and I do encourage you to seek it out – but this taster should give you an idea:

> And I shall spend my pension on brandy and summer gloves
> And satin sandals, and say we've no money for butter.
> I shall sit down on the pavement when I am tired
> And gobble up samples in shops and press alarm bells
> And run my stick along the public railings
> And make up for the sobriety of my youth.

It goes on in the same vein, so ebulliently it makes you start to look forward to growing older and throwing off the social strictures of middle youth, where to dress 'inappropriately' could have a negative impact on your job prospects, your children, or your chance of finding a new partner.

What Jenny Joseph and the lady sitting next to me in the hairdresser have both realised is that in style terms, old age is not a restriction, but the start of a new freedom. As Noel Coward so deftly put it: 'It doesn't matter how bold you are when the dangerous age is past.'

Now, that is something to look forward to.

Knicker elastic

When I was a child, I was often confused by references in books to knicker elastic and the breaking thereof. This was an event that led to terribly embarrassing moments featuring said knickers around ankles. I could see that it wouldn't be a good look, but I didn't really understand the mechanism of how it happened.

My own undies must have had elastic in them somewhere, I reckoned, but not the kind that could break. They just sort of got baggier over time. An equally mystifying concept was that of putting one's hankie up one's knicker leg. I tried it a few times and it just fell out again as soon as I walked. It wasn't until much later that I realised that the school knickers in question were more like brushed cotton pantaloons with elastic around the legs, as well as around the waist. It must have made a nice little storage area.

But forget knicker legs – by the time my own daughter is reading (I hope) Noel Streatfeild and Elizabeth Enright and E Nesbit and all the authors I adored as a youngster, I think even the idea of a handkerchief will be weird.

We have already come upon them, actually, in *The Tale of Mrs Tiggy-Winkle*, one of our favourites in the Beatrix Potter canon (she's very keen on the idea of a talking hedgehog). I don't think she has any idea what little Lucie's lost 'pocket-handkins' are, so it's not an issue at this point, but I'm sure it will be one day. I can imagine the conversation:

Peggy: 'What's a handkin?'
Me: 'It's short for handkerchief, which was a small piece of cotton that people used to carry around to blow their noses on.'
P: 'Like a tissue?'
M: 'Yes, except we used to wash them and iron them after we'd used them, and then use them again.'
P: 'Yucky!'

I do wonder if anyone uses a proper hankie any more. Everyone did when I was a child; I used to iron my father's, making sure the embroidered 'D' was always on top when I put them away in the drawer.

I still have loads of my own – they were considered a suitable present for a child in the 1960s. Can you imagine the reaction if you gave a twenty-first-century kid a box of initialled hankies for their birthday? They'd probably beat you to death with their games console. I've still got my hankies – in special little embroidered pochettes that my grandmother gave me – and I look at them occasionally, but I don't ever use them.

All this makes me wonder what other items that have seemed everyday in my lifetime will become – or already are – as archaic as a crinoline.

I can think of at least two things from my own youth that, for my daughter's sake, I am very glad have already gone the way of the dodo: itchy wool and Bri-Nylon. Both of them created garments like mobile torture chambers for children. There was a particular family holiday which was blighted for my brother Nick by a pair of ferociously itchy wool trousers. Just reminding my mother of it can reduce her to tears of laughter. He still doesn't find it amusing.

In my own case, I can remember a red-and-white deckchair-stripe summer dress made from 100 per cent Bri-Nylon. It was so completely impermeable it might as well have been made from PVC and my mother was thrilled – it was a homemade number – because the fabric didn't fray. You could just cut it like a plastic bin liner. On a hot summer day, it was like wearing one, too.

So while I certainly don't mourn the passing of such items from everyday life into a footnote in the history of costume, it is unsettling to realise that my own childhood is fast becoming what I used to call 'the olden days'.

Well worn

After giving the matter serious thought – every time I look in the mirror – I have reached a new understanding about ageing. My conclusion is this: it is better to let it wither you than turn you into a hamster-chopped eyes-wide-shut freak-head (those considering surgery, take note).

There is a way of ageing naturally and still being beautiful – you just have to get used to the idea of beauty in the style of a Roman ruin, rather than a freshly blooming rose.

The word for it is 'patina'. People can develop a pleasing patina, just like garden urns softened by lichen, Dutch old masters warmed by centuries of tobacco residue, French provincial tables pleasantly hatchet scarred and vintage handbags polished by decades of warm hands on the leather.

But while I have always loved a bit of crackle glaze on an old jug, I admit it's taken me a while to appreciate this kind of beauty in human form. I can remember, years ago on a big photo shoot in Los Angeles, being really shocked to see my beauty editor colleague sticking her face towards the mid-day sun with no SPF on.

'Aren't you worried about sun damage?' I asked from beneath the very wide brim of my hat and a mime artist covering of Factor 30.

'No,' she said. 'I want to get wrinkles. I want to look like Georgia O'Keeffe.'

At the time I thought she was nuts – and I still wouldn't advise such cavalier solar exposure for the obvious health reasons – but over time I have come to see the point of that kind of beauty.

Georgia O'Keeffe's visage was as cracked and lined as the New Mexico desert landscape that so inspired her, but with her hair pulled back, her eyes twinkling with intelligent amusement, she looked amazing. Her face was like a relief map of the fascinating life she had led.

In the same way, I have a friend in his nineties who is simply one of the most beautiful men I have ever met. His face is all cheekbones and crevices, bright blue eyes sparking out at you.

When Paul smiles, his skin breaks up and pieces of his face move around, like continental plates shifting, and his shock of straight white hair sets it all off a treat. I have no idea if he was amazingly handsome in his youth – although I suspect he was – and it doesn't matter, because the point is how marvellous-looking he is now.

Keith Richards is another example of this kind of weathered beauty, achieved thirty years younger through serious hard living, and it is interesting to see it starting to develop in people at an even earlier stage.

The chaps in the re-formed Take That are great examples (although I would say that, because I do love them so . . .). But even putting aside my pathetic adolescent passion for them, I think Mark and Jason, in particular, look better now they are proper wrinkly men than they did in their peach-cheeked boy band phase. Their faces look slept in, which is a good thing in a man.

Well, maybe not so good in fellow Take That-er Gary Barlow. He's the one who writes all the great songs and he looks more like Elton John every time I see him. Maybe it's all those hours at the piano, but life – or genetics – can be such a bitch, because as Jason and Mark get fabulously haggard, Gary is getting stocky and jowly.

Wrinkly jowly faces just don't look beautiful the way wrinkly bony ones do, and that is the problem with aspiring to this patina beauty. You have to be thin to pull it off. It's all about jutting cheekbones and deep-set eyes.

So just when I thought I'd got the better of it, there goes ageing one mean-minded sonofabitch step ahead of me again. It's going to be even more important to be thin at seventy than it was at twenty-five. Damn.

Waist of space

I think I am going to have to buy myself a hula hoop. Because isn't hula-hooping supposed to be the best way to whittle down your waist?

Not that I have ever been able to keep a hoop hula-ing for more than a millisecond. I always start out full of hope, sending it off on its first whirl with a great flourish, then waggling my hips like a crazed belly dancer, but the damn hoop always ends up by my feet the moment I let go of it.

Despite these setbacks I'm sure I could learn to hula-hoop if I were desperate enough – and I am desperate, having just spent five very lowering minutes flicking through the Burberry look book for next season. It's all belts. I'm not kidding, there is a belt in every single outfit. Coats, cardigans, jackets, jumpers, day dresses, cocktail dresses, tuxedo pants – *men's* tuxedo pants – they all have belts. Even the belts have belts.

There are all different kinds – wide belts, skinny belts, ribbon belts, elastic belts, tied belts, buckled belts, chain belts – but with one dreadful thing in common: they are all worn neatly around the waist.

Now, I was mad about those late nineties/early noughties belts – the ones that hid a multitude of sins, hanging low on the hip, just where the tummy can be dodgy. Those belts were my friends. Especially the ones that were made of woven leather so they didn't have a nasty little hierarchy of holes to remind you what level of a fat day you were having. But these belts are the enemy. These are the kind of belts which didn't even suit me when I was young and skinny, and now I'm back in belt Siberia.

Of course, I could just shrug and say, 'Hey, so no Burberry ready-to-wear for me this season, then' (like I could ever afford it). But the thing is, at the moment, whatever Burberry designer Christopher Bailey says pretty much goes. He doesn't single-handedly set the fashion agenda (Stefano Pilati at YSL is doing that these days), but Mr Bailey is a very good barometer of it. He seems to know exactly which key elements to take and use within the slightly limited Burberry repertoire.

And the really maddening thing is I love the new collection. It's gorgeous. If I were rich I would want to buy it all, and as things are, I would look forward to buying a few good chain-store rip-offs ('interpretations'), but I won't be doing either because I just can't wear a waist-defining belt.

So I reckon I have to make a considered decision on this issue. Having accepted that waist-sitting belts of all kinds are probably the key fashion trend for the next year or so, here are what I see as my options:

- Plastic surgery. I'd have to have a breast reduction, several ribs removed and extra length put into my legs. Next.
- Lose fourteen kilos. Well, I would look better in a belt if I didn't have a spare tyre on either side of it, but when you are short with a 'womanly' bosom, I don't think anything that cuts you in half is ever going to look good. Also I would have absolutely no hips or buttocks at that weight. I'd look like a human wedge of brie. Pointy-end down. With a belt on.
- Ignore the fashion trend. Now that is a radical option, but one I have absolutely no intention of taking. I already feel left out. I want to play too.
- Find a cunning way to make the look work for me. Now, I think there just might be something I can do with a narrow belt over a light knit and then a cropped jacket over the top . . . I think it could work.

Or I could just wear a hula hoop as a belt.

Letting go

I have been pondering a lot recently on the subject of letting yourself go. Or, as you more usually hear it, the phrase 'She's really let herself go.' It's funny, but I don't think I've ever heard anyone say that about themselves, or about a man. It's a judgement that is laid down on women, usually by other women.

Working at home, as I do at the moment, I am all too aware of the possibility of someone saying it about me sometime soon. When you work alone, at an activity where comfort is paramount (you try sitting at a computer for ten hours in tight pants), there is all too strong a temptation to drift through the day in socks, pyjamas and a cardigan, hair pulled back into the de rigeur scruffy ponytail.

It gets worse: this outfit can then all too easily be worn to the corner shop with just a raincoat over the top and Birkenstocks on the feet. Adding to the general effect, your hair might not be washed quite often enough and make-up becomes something for high days and holidays. What is this thing you call lipstick?

It takes something hideous like bumping into an ex-lover or, even worse, an ex-love *rival* in this state to realise that you have allowed yourself to turn from a butterfly back into a bug.

But despite the fact I am sitting here, pretty much as described above, I don't think I have really let myself go. This is just deep scruffiness; it's nothing that can't easily be corrected by a quick hairwash and blow-dry, a bit of slap, some tailoring, a tasty pair of high heels, a swipe of MAC lippie and a squirt of Calèche. That would take me half an hour, max.

Letting yourself go properly takes a lot more commitment. I don't think someone can really be said to have let themselves go until they have reached the point that scrubbing them up would take days, if not months, to achieve.

For one thing, serious weight gain is always a major part of a proper letting-go. Weight gain that has gone way beyond those few pesky extra kilos into actual obesity. But fat is just part of it. Hair is left to rack and ruin, allowed to grow long and wild, with grey roots. Skin is left to return to nature, as is superfluous hair of all kinds, including that on the chin, often growing out of a fat wart. Yes, letting go is the apotheosis of all crimes against our worst fattist, ageist, looks-ist prejudices. And that is why I think there is something almost glorious in it.

Last summer I was staying in a small coastal town which

seemed to have attracted an unusual proportion of women in this state. They waddled along the street, with the pro-verbial spare tyres – but actual size – visibly rolling beneath their jersey clothes.

And that was one of the things I loved about them. They had let go to such an extent they didn't even bother with any of the desperate camouflage clothing most women resort to before they quite give up – the almost-chic elastic-waist linen pants and hip-skimming tops.

No such compromises for these girls; they were letting it all hang out, many of them in tight jersey leggings and quite a few in shorts – probably because the cut of those garments prevented their mighty thighs chafing together. Many of them broke that other commandment of female allure and walked along the road eating huge ice-creams.

After experiencing an initial knee-jerk horror response – 'Who *are* these people?' – I was mad about them. They were like a super-race of Andrea Dworkins who didn't play by the rules. I like to think that they hadn't let themselves go, with all the lazy passivity that term implies; they had simply let go. As in let go of all the imposed 'shoulds' women allow ourselves to suffer under.

'She's really let go' has quite a different ring to it, don't you think?

Slap and tickle

I was stolidly pressing concealer onto my cheeks the other day when it suddenly struck me: I no longer gaily dust on my make-up to enhance my features; I use it to *build* my face, like a character actor or a drag queen.

No wonder they call it slap. Time was when cosmetics caressed my face with a light touch; now it's more like the back of a hand across my chops as I pile it on in layers.

Like all the major landmarks of ageing I have experienced so far, I acknowledged this shift with a sudden, punch-to-the-guts lurch. One minute it seemed getting ready to face the world meant a whisk of blusher, a stroke of eye shadow, a quick once-over with lip pencil and gloss, a lick of mascara and off we go. Foundation was only for special occasions.

Now I have to use two kinds of concealer. One to cover the red marks of rosacea (I think that's what it is) on my cheeks and chin; the other to erase the dark shadows under and around my eyes. Then it's foundation over the top to even out the impasto.

The smudgy eye pencil that used to be an occasional diversion is now essential to cover up the persistent cysts on the roots of my lower lashes, which the eye specialist has counselled me to leave be.

I have long used a corrective, flesh-coloured pencil to even out lips rendered slightly irregular by (non-cosmetic) surgery, so that's nothing new, but the constant moisturising of the lip area to prevent the hen's arse look is.

The cheek colour that used to be like a warm kiss (such a well-named product, 'blusher'), is now more like a restorative, breathing life back into the cadaver and giving a look of plumpness to the sag.

Eye shadow that I used to stroke on boldly for what I thought was a fetching Greta Garbo effect now disappears into the pachyderm folds of my eye sockets unless applied to exactly the right spot.

But while that all sounds pretty gloomy, it's really not all depressing. It is true that make-up has moved from optional to essential status in my life, but there is an upside: I am fascinated by its transformative powers.

The state of my skin, in particular, does require leaving a little more time than before to get ready to go out – even to post a letter – but every time I go through that routine, I step back from the mirror amazed. I look so different after I've done it. I hope I don't look as overtly made up as the aforementioned drag queen, but the transformation is still pretty extraordinary.

Thanks to the advice of my beauty editor best pal, I think

the concealers do their job without too loudly advertising their presence. And if they don't, will somebody please tell me? (I once had a business lunch with a woman who had one of those rings of unblended foundation – the ones beauty writers are always warning us about – around her jaw and I could not look at, or think about, anything else for the entire meal. I still wonder if I should have said something.)

But unless I am completely deluding myself, I think my made-up face looks pretty natural. I mean, it still looks like make-up, but not, I think, like cake-up. And it makes me realise how very lucky we women are to have its magical, alchemical properties at our disposal.

I can entirely see what drag queens get out of the process. They have a weapon denied all other men (give or take the odd Liberace), which means that with the deft application of some trowels of slap they can transform themselves into someone else.

And with warm fingertips and some overpriced concealer, I can transform myself back into me.

Strangers on a train

I really must stop staring at people on trains, but I just can't help it. People are so interesting. I love seeing what they are wearing and wondering why they have chosen that particular outfit for that particular day. This can keep me amused for hours. Really, I enjoy it much more than watching television.

Just the other morning I got absolutely fixated on two women sitting just opposite me. One was a little older than the other – in her sixties, I would say. The other was mid- to late fifties. The thing that got me staring and obsessing was that the older one was very much the chicer and I considered it my pressing duty to analyse why.

She'd done her own hair, I could tell, on rollers, and she did the tinting herself too, I decided. It looked very nice, but it didn't have the polish of a hairdresser's professional touch. It was a 1950s sort of style, quite short, perky curls, but in a good way; not a sad, time-warp hairdo.

She was nicely made up, with a bold lip, which always

endears a gal to me (as long as it's not fluoro pink). This was a sophisticated, deep mid-red that spoke to me of someone who knows how to mix a drink. I was liking this woman more with every moment.

And I really loved her outfit. She had on the simplest black pants and cardigan with some very nice statement beads, which she wore with perfect insouciance. It looked like she'd had them a long time. They really belonged to her.

Another piquant note was a pashmina in a very good red – and red is a difficult colour to get right – that was perfect with her lipstick. She also knew how to drape it artlessly round her neck while she was seated, a skill in itself.

But what really made me super-keen on this woman is that when we got to our destination, she got up and put on a *black* coat – and then a *brown* bag. That totally made her outfit for me.

A black bag would have been way too matchy-matchy, something to avoid in general, but even more so when you are working back a red-and-black ensemble, which can so easily turn you into a walking riddle. (What is black and white and red all over? A newspaper – or an overly natty outfit.)

The final touch that made me want to hand her my business card and suggest we meet up sometime for a Negroni and a hand or two of kaluki was that she put the brown bag on bandolero-style, across her body.

That's how I always wear my favourite brown bag. By this time I felt we were practically related. A feeling which only increased when I clocked her simple black patent leather loafers. This was a woman up from the sticks for the day, and dressed to take on the big city – but entirely on her own terms.

Her friend, on the other hand, was wearing kitten-heel shoes. Very pretty, but if you've ever spent a day mincing along on those tiny heels, you'll know how irritating they quickly become. She really had a much better bag than her pal, too. It was a very nice red tote, but wedged on over the shoulder of her slightly too-bulky black-and-white coat, it troubled me. I knew that bag would be slipping off her shoulder all day long. Or weighing her down on one side when she finally resorted to carrying it in her hand. Meanwhile her friend would be strolling blithely along with her hands-free bandolero bag and her comfortable shoes.

As we went our separate ways on the station platform I completed my analysis and concluded that when it comes to style, having the confidence to be comfortable always wins over trying too hard.

Foot soldiers

I sometimes feel we are living in a culture so decadent it makes the last days of ancient Rome seem as restrained as a Shaker barn raising.

There's bare flesh on open display everywhere, filth all over advertising billboards, hideous spam porno in your email inbox and endless ghastly reality TV shows that celebrate all the worst human characteristics – avarice, envy, selfishness, competitiveness, wind etc.

Then I open American *Vogue* and read an article about women who have cosmetic surgery – on their feet. Not elective surgery to relieve painful conditions such as bunions, ingrown toenails, or plantar warts, but completely inessential vanity surgery to make their feet look nicer.

'I got tired of burying my toes in the sand when I went to the beach. It was humiliating,' says a 37-year-old sales consultant quoted in the article. A woman who clearly has far too much time to think about herself.

The crime nature had committed against her? Her

second toes were longer than her first. But not after Dr David Ostad had gone in and shaved 2 mm of bone off the second knuckle of said blighted toes. Feeling sick yet? Not Ms MeMeMe; she's thrilled with it all. 'The transformation is amazing and I was back in high heels in two months.' Well, thank GOD. She must have felt like the Elephant Woman of East Hampton before the op.

'More aristocratic, less peasant-like,' was the request from an unnamed actress to another New York plastic surgeon with regard to her own clodhoppers, which were clearly the only thing between her and an Academy Award.

The surgeon was happy to oblige (beach house, beach house, beach house) and promptly lengthened her toes with bone-grafting techniques, removed soft tissue from her instep to narrow her feet and administered fat injections to hide unsightly veins and tendons.

Is there something wrong with me that I find this outrageously vain and self-indulgent? Am I the only mealy-mouthed, self-righteous do-gooder who thinks that the good doctor's bone-grafting skills could be better used by landmine-maimed children in Africa than by spoiled thespians in Manhattan?

Not that I'm unsympathetic to women who dislike their own feet. I have several friends who long to wear strappy shoes in summer but feel they can't, because they have less than lovely tootsies. Rather as I would love to wear skimpy little sundresses and feel I can't because of my overcatered mammary glands. But you get on with it, don't you? You ack-sen-chu-ate the positive and move on.

Not these self-obsessed, over-indulged New York nugget-heads. Consultant podiatrist Suzanne Levine DPM, who, it says in the article, 'regularly performs surgery in her three-and-a-half-inch Manolos', also offers a service where she injects collagen into the balls of people's feet so that they will find high heels less excruciatingly uncomfortable.

'Designer high heels like Sergio Rossis may be gorgeous,' says Dr Levine, someone I would very much like to slap. 'But they're very slight-soled. As you age, your feet become less plump, making these delicate shoes less and less comfortable to wear.'

Fine. So stop wearing them.

And it doesn't end with the collagen. After they've had these various foot-perfecting procedures (and probably Botox to get rid of those life-threatening ankle wrinkles), Dr Levine's clients then return each month for foot facials (hello?) which cost US$225 a time. This makes me so cross the top of my head is itching.

It's not that I'm resentful of people having more money than me – so much money they can throw it away on foot facials – or so much spare time they can spend an afternoon a month just having their feet massaged; it's the overwhelming obsession with the self I find so repugnant.

Come to think of it, they wore sandals all the time in Ancient Rome, didn't they? I wonder if Caligula ever had a foot facial.

Comfortably Middle-Aged

Many times I have bewailed the unavoidable stepping stones of the ageing process. But having now stepped from First Grey Hair, on to First Deep Wrinkle and, via Chin Bristle, to Sagging Knees, I find that I have reached some kind of island where I can rest for a while before moving on to the next stage (which probably includes HRT and Hip Replacement). I'm thinking of it as Comfortably Middle-Aged.

Which doesn't mean giving up and giving in to elastic waistbands and easy-care shortie hairdos, but just a state of contented acceptance. Which is actually a much more pleasant place to reside than Glorious Youth ever was.

Here are a few pointers which will enable you to recognise whether you have reached the same plateau:

- You wear the same make-up look every day.
- You don't plan on trying a new hairstyle any time soon.
- You can get quite excited by a new roll of zip-lock bags.

- There are certain cosmetic items that you have repeat-purchased countless times.
- You still buy anti-ageing creams, but you really do know it's all nonsense.
- You seriously can't remember where you bought quite a few of your clothes and accessories.
- You've had some of them over twenty years and still going strong.
- You'll never wear a miniskirt again and you couldn't care less.
- You don't feel remotely self-conscious in your sunhat.
- You've had your watch longer than you've had your car.
- You sometimes hold up your face at the sides, while you are looking in the bathroom mirror, to see what you would look like after a facelift.
- Ditto: breasts.
- You want to find out more about those injections that make fat rolls melt away, but aren't a surgical procedure.
- You really can't believe that you ever weighed under fifty kilos.
- You travel with your own pillow.
- You travel with your own tea bags.
- You travel with your own little kettle or water-heating element so you're never very far from a hot beverage.
- You own a flask for transporting same and use it, in public, with no sense of shame.
- You're thingy about which mug you have.
- That's enough milk!

- You haven't had sugar in tea or coffee for years.
- You haven't smoked for years.
- None of the guests at your dinner parties seem to smoke anymore.
- You can stop after one glass of wine.
- Now just remind me – what is a bikini wax?
- You don't know which single – or album – is Number One.
- But you do know which non-fiction book is.
- In a hotel room you'll turn to CNN before MTV.
- You love and worship your digital camera, but you're still working up to an iPod.
- You've got CDs which you also own on cassette and vinyl.
- You hop up and down with rage if anyone retunes your radio away from Radio National.
- You look at the 'Your Money' section of the paper first.
- You open bank statements as soon as they arrive.
- You care about the interest rates the way you used to care who was Number One.
- You've got friends who are grandparents.
- You've been to a fiftieth birthday party. And it wasn't your dad's.
- Morning tea is a more enticing event than happy hour.
- You don't like the look of that Angelina Jolie.
- You can't believe how young Scarlett Johansson is.
- You really, really hate dance music.
- Now 'Car Wash' – that's dance music.

- You are constantly amazed at how beautiful The Young are.
- You sometimes feel like a filthy old perve when a particularly glorious young man/woman walks by.
- You are starting to feel a bit queasy at the thought of watching *Death in Venice* ever again, although you loved it when you were twenty.
- You still get just as excited as you ever did about a new pair of shoes.

Mini ha ha

We need to talk about miniskirts. Fashion designers seem determined to make us all wear shorter hemlines again, so the issue must be addressed.

Now, obviously this development is heaven for young gels (not to mention men of all ages). After a winter of pants, it really is the most wonderful feeling of freedom to let your legs roam free. I always know when it's spring because the day comes when I absolutely can't bear the idea of putting trousers on, it has to be a skirt. I just wish it could still be a really short skirt, as it was in my younger days, because although I will still wear a shortish skirt with black opaques, there is no way I will be going around in a mini with bare legs on display.

But I do seriously wonder why I have bought into this self-imposed bit of fashion ageism, because really there is only one thing to say about women over forty wearing miniskirts: Anna Wintour.

The carpaccio-slim editor-in-chief of American *Vogue*

adores short skirts. She's got great legs, she likes to show them off and it suits her. And she definitely won't see the lower side of fifty again. Fashion's ultimate authority must be thrilled that the world's designers have now rejoined her higher on the thigh, at a level not seen since the 1980s.

What Ms Wintour understands is that great legs are the ultimate status symbol, because they are just about the only physical asset that can't be achieved through surgery. You can have saddlebags sucked off the thighs and coarse hair lasered into oblivion, but I have never read a reference to ankle-refining. And while I have heard, with my own ears, Russian model agents talking about leg-lengthening, I don't believe it's a widely available cosmetic procedure.

The thing is, breasts can be faked, faces can be lifted, eyes can be almond-ised and even feet can be narrowed, but great shins are bred in the bone. Remember Princess Di's heavenly racehorse shanks? Generations of selective breeding. Just like Phar Lap.

Which is why women like the late New York socialite Nan Kempner love to get their skinny legs out and about. In fact, one of the defining characteristics of that city's 'Social X-Rays' – a group of which she was the doyenne – is tiny legs, like bony hair grips. They're as much an essential credential for membership of that feminine elite as the Sutton Place townhouse and the solitaire diamond the size of a hazelnut.

The other great thing about legs is that give or take a few troublesome veins – which can now be effectively zapped – you've got them for life. OK, your knees do go a bit like a fallen soufflé at a certain point, but as long as you don't put on much weight it's not a complete disaster. In fact, those kind of scrawny, wrinkly knees, which Kate Moss is starting to develop, have an attractiveness of their own, rather like Michael Palin's crinkly laugh lines.

So while after a certain age you may no longer feel it is appropriate to flaunt your exhausted dugs (and I speak personally here), your upper arms may resemble chicken wings and your abdomen might be blancmange, finely turned ankles and calves remain so and can still be aired and shared with aplomb.

Just ask the original *Cosmo* girl, Helen Gurley Brown. She's well over eighty and still wears her Diane von Furstenberg dresses slashed way up on the thigh. With high heels. Gets away with it, too.

So if you were lucky enough to be born with a dainty ankle, or an elegant knee, now is your time to flaunt it. I just wish I felt able to take my own advice on this.

Revenge Wear

There's daywear, there's evening wear, there's resort, formal, smart casual and suitable attire for the races, but my favourite clothing code of all is Revenge Wear.

I was reminded of this oft-neglected category the other day when I saw a picture of Angelina Jolie accompanied by the – bold-face type – caption, 'BRANGELINA – SHE MOVES OUT!!!'

Apparently she and Brad just ain't getting on – she wants to go and live in Africa full time, Brad's not so keen, she knows he's been talking to Jen and she's moved out, so there. It's probably all utter scuttlebutt, but, oh my, the picture was perfect to illustrate it.

She's wearing a tightly knotted trench coat and dark glasses, and her hair is scraped back. She looks slightly strained and wan – under her masterful no-make-up make-up – but achingly beautiful, with cheekbones standing out like flying buttresses. It's one of the best Revenge Wear looks I have ever seen.

As Angelina clearly understands, the key to it is to put over the idea that you have suffered and are still suffering, but to look absolutely gorgeous at the same time. So the man who has caused you all this angst will feel: a) terribly guilty for making you so sad and b) mad with desire for you.

And if he has accidentally been having it away with someone else he will really regret it when he sees how beautiful you are and realise he has made a horrible mistake and he'll never see her again and he'll buy you a big diamond and move with you to Africa and the other woman will tragically fall off a cliff and that will be the end of *her*.

That's the way women can tend to think when they are in the frame of mind which leads to Revenge Wear being assumed. It's not an entirely rational state – which makes it all the more fascinating

Until the Brangelina pic the best revenge look I had seen was sported by a playwright I used to know. She had written a play, her partner was directing it and I was in it (I was a bit of an actorine back in the day). In a gap between the first staging of the production and its revival for the Edinburgh Festival, this golden couple split up. Which was very sad.

The playwright took herself – and her pain – off to stay with her grandmother in Italy, returning just in time for the first rehearsal. We were in a tatty church hall in Leith when she made her entrance – which remains quite the best I have ever witnessed.

She sort of fell through the door wearing a black trench coat – clearly the Revenge Wear classic – the belt knotted even more tightly than Angelina's, showing off just quite how extraordinarily skinny she had become, huge black sunglasses revealing just enough of her face to show she had the most spectacular suntan. It was masterly and the director was lost for words – result!

It was so stagy, hilariously steeped in French film noir and old Joan Crawford movies, but it worked. They got back together almost immediately and then she made him suffer, as only an Italian woman could.

I had actually tried the Revenge Wear thing once myself, a few years before I witnessed that masterclass. I was eighteen, my so-cool looked-like-Bryan-Ferry saxophonist boyfriend had dumped me for some ghastly tart and I was heartbroken. I took to my bed and really couldn't eat. I got brilliantly thin.

Eventually I got up and the evening came around when it was time to go out again. I knew I would see him at a particular nightclub and boy did I work it, putting together an Antony Price tribute outfit (he used to dress Jerry Hall in the Roxy Music era . . .) that maximised my new skinniness. It had the desired effect – his eyes nearly came out on stalks, the new gf looked sick – but it didn't work. He stuck with her.

If only I'd known about the trench coat.

Small is beautiful

Fortunate as we are to live in a country where clean drinking water can be taken for granted – droughts willing and give or take the odd stray *E coli* – I am a great believer in making the most of the little pleasantnesses of life. We are so lucky to have them.

Take for example, cotton wool balls. I know they are a stupidly expensive way of buying something you use only to take off eye make-up and then throw in the bin. They also take up a lot of storage space, but every time I open the little basket by my bathroom basin to remove said caked-on mascara, it gives me a mini-hit of pleasure to see them there.

Sometimes I even buy the pastel-coloured ones that are supposed to be the last word in suburban naffness. I don't care, I like them. They are fluffy and pretty and camp and they cheer me up. They are the Ziegfeld Follies of cotton wool. I have in lean times bought one of those brutal cotton wool bales like giant tampons, and have hated it afresh every time I came to use it.

I feel the same way about sugar cubes. The very idea of them makes me smile. In fact, I like to have a quite a wardrobe of sugar styles at my disposal. As well as the obvious icing, golden castor, and castor in a jar with vanilla pods for baking, I have cubes to serve with tea (I'd love some tongs) and those sexy sugar crystals for after-dinner coffee. I have a secret hankering for some of those little sticks with sugar crystals encrusting the end, but that might be going a bit too far, even for me.

Other fetishes I group under the pleasantness heading are nice soap, always changed before it becomes a slimy communion wafer, hot water bottle covers (mine are Toile de Jouy) and fresh cloth napkins for every dinner. I don't understand people's resistance to that little finesse. Really, how hard it is to throw a few napkins in the washer?

I also confess that I love those tiny little paper napkins with lovely prints on them, such as old blue-and-white tea cups. Paper napkins are one of the ultimate 'non-u' items of that snobby English system of 'u' and 'non-u' (the 'u' denoted 'upper class') and I would never put them out for dinner, but for afternoon tea? I love them. And if you came to my house around Christmas, you would probably have one with a poinsettia print on it to go with your mince pie.

These little luxuries are nothing to do with being posh or pretentious or rich – it's not about having five different Sèvres dinner services and solid silver Christofle cutlery, although I would love to, of course. I don't think I am in any way better than the next person because I have lavender bags in all my drawers that emit the most lovely waft every time I get out a pair of socks; it is just an enjoyment of tiny harmless details which make life just a little more delightful.

Of course, this all comes under the terrible crime of being 'genteel' and bourgeois. In fact, I am probably bordering on the full Hyacinth Bucket, but I don't care. These little gestures are my barricades against the hideous cruelty, injustice, deprivation and suffering that spews out at us every day from the front pages and the TV news.

It doesn't mean I don't think about those things and rail against them. Pleasantness is not an ostrich option – it's more a matter of acknowledging the good fortune to be on the outside of the ghastliness looking in.

And so I live by this mantra: *Do* sweat the small stuff.

Joan Collins Fan Club

Want a bit of good news about getting older? Thought you might. Well, I can sum it up in two words: Joan Collins.

I recently had an audience with Miss Collins and it was a revelation. It wasn't just the two of us; there was Madame Lipgloss up on stage and a packed theatre of *Dynasty* fanatics, drag queens, general stalkers and the simply curious (that was me).

Short of holding her down and carbon-dating her leg, I don't think we are ever going to find out Miss C's real age (although 1933 has been mentioned in regard to birth dates). But judging by what she was wearing in the adorable toddler photos with which she opened her auto-biographical one-woman show, she can't be too many eggs short of a basket of eighty.

Strutting about on a fine pair of heels, wearing the kind of internally engineered, body-hugging gown favoured by Marlene Dietrich in her later years, she looked divatastic.

The wigs have always helped, of course, adding an

element of artifice that is the very essence of true Holly-wood glamour. Because when you know someone only via celluloid, cathode or Kodak, seeing them in natural real life can only disappoint without it. Unless there's something properly phoney going on, you're not quite convinced by them.

Anyway, Joanie C looked amazing for her age, with the help of the rug and the NASA corsetry, plus her apparently undintable self-belief (and she fervently denies that she has ever had cosmetic surgery). But what really struck me as we progressed through her decades, with a slideshow to accom-pany her deliciously camp anecdotes, was the age at which she had been her most beautiful.

It wasn't when she was a ravishing RADA-graduate teen, like a cross between Elizabeth Taylor and Audrey Hepburn, with a bit of Gina Lollobrigida thrown in. It wasn't even when she was a Rank starlet, or better still, a full-on Holly-wood one, signed to Twentieth Century Fox and chatting casually to Marilyn Monroe at Bel Air parties. It was in her middle to late thirties, after she'd had her children. This cheered me up so much.

There was one particular picture of Mrs Newley with the three kids (actually that would have made her Mrs Kass — what-ever), wearing some kind of 1970s silk kaftan top, where she just looked drop-dead fabulous. Her face was all elegant angles and even her arms looked especially beautiful.

Now, I believe that when some women have babies a specific metabolic change occurs, dissolving the last baby fat from their faces to reveal the structure beneath. So if you've got great bones like Joan, you start to look like a goddess. Not just pretty – properly beautiful. And this segue into a truly elegant womanhood is not restricted to mothers. I've also seen it in childless girlfriends who have finally found settled happiness in a relationship.

Of course, a sense of romantic and domestic security can send some people off into a treacherous twin sofa/ trackie dak/pizza delivery downward spiral, but for those of a Joan Collins constitution it seems to bring out their true radiance, almost as though they finally feel safe enough to let their best selves shine out. It's a mature form of beauty, which I think is much more fascinating than the poignant first bud kind.

The really good news is that while Joan's relationship situations were a bit patchy after that glowing yummy mummy stage, the mature beauty stuck around long enough to re-launch her as the TV superstar we so loved in the 1980s.

And now, of course, she drinks deep of the ultimate elixir of youth – she has a much younger husband. We all have a lot to learn from Miss Collins.

All buttoned up

Do you have a button box? I only ask as I wonder, in this new world of disposable clothes, whether anybody keeps buttons any more.

I have one, but it is more of a container for those little plastic bags of spare buttons that come with better clothes, rather than for ones thriftily snipped off old shirts before their conversion into silver-polishing cloths, as in days of ancient yore, ie my childhood.

I always put those posh buttons carefully away, even though I've never actually used any of them. It's just nice to know they're there. In case. And apart from anything else, I was delighted to find a use for the lovely old Chanel box I keep them in, which was far too beautiful to throw away. It's just the right size for buttons.

My mum has button tins, rather than boxes: a Cadbury's cocoa tin for shirt buttons and a larger toffee tin for buttons, general. The cocoa tin and contents were actually my grandmother's, which means it could be over eighty years old and any of the buttons in it much older, which is quite a thought.

In a nice link down the decades, my mum recently gave both tins to my sister, a serious needlewoman – a genetic inheritance from my master dressmaker grandmother which passed me and my mum right on by. We can both labour with a needle if we have to, but it makes us cross and itchy. My mum does a nice line in trousers shortened to two dif-ferent leg lengths, while my specialty is sewing on buttons with threads that knot and tangle in mid-pull.

In all honesty, just thinking about sewing gives me the screaming ab dabs, but I used to love playing with those button tins. On rainy afternoons I would take myself off to the cupboard on the landing where all my grandmother's sewing stuff was kept and get the tins out.

I can remember the sound of them, the smell of them and the feel of them. The rattle of the tins and then the small roar of the buttons onto the carpet. The combination of metal, plastic, mother-of-pearl, wood and bone created a unique scent. They felt slippery and cold running through my fingers and it was strangely satisfying just to stir them around in the tin.

When I saw the film of *Oscar and Lucinda* I really related to the part where the stern clergyman father comments on Oscar's activities with pebbles. 'You have changed your taxonomy,' he says, or words to that effect, continuing that they used to be sorted by size and now they were sorted by colour. That's what I used to do with the buttons.

First I'd match them up into groups of the same kind, then I'd mix them all up and put them into groups by colour. Later I might make a long line of them in ascending size. That was generally the mixed tin. Exploration of the shirt button tin was much more specialised as they were a myriad of tiny variations on a theme of small and white.

It was much more of a challenge to sort them into types and I can remember getting quite mesmerised by the very fine ones made of real mother-of-pearl. I used to end up just staring at individual buttons and wondering where they came from.

Next time I visit my sister I must have a look at those tins, as I'm sure I would still remember individual buttons. They're a family heirloom, really, and I know I'm not the only person who feels that way.

A friend of mine inherited the family button tin from a great-aunt and sewed them all over the front of a waistcoat, like a pearly king's. It is a most magical garment.

So if you don't already have a button tin, perhaps you should consider starting one, for posterity. Or just for rainy afternoons.

The wardrobe diet

I have just discovered something absolutely terrible. Or absolutely great, depending how you look at it. To explain – I am writing from the fashion shows in Milan. This is a situation which normally inspires me to unburden my agonies about getting dressed when you are going to spend your day looking at the world's most beautiful women, surrounded by the world's chicest women.

This season I have uncovered the key to it all and it is so simple it makes me want to weep: I have lost weight. That's it; that was all I needed to do to make something terribly difficult terribly easy.

And I haven't even lost loads of weight – I'm not yet ready to sell my before-and-after pictures to a slimming club – but just four kilos is enough to make putting together an outfit a pleasure rather than the problem it had become.

Now it is a matter of choosing what I *want* to wear, rather than desperately scrabbling to find some wretched thing I *can* wear without feeling hopelessly less-than when faced with an audience of 1,854 slim, elegant fashion editors and buyers (the other 146 are the chubby ones).

In fact, I was nearly late this morning because I had almost too much choice for what to put on. Should I wear the grey flannel pencil skirt with my cashmere twinset and pearls for a bit of a Louis Vuitton ice-maiden moment? Or should I go with the hipster Chloé pants and studded belt for more of a rock-chick thing?

I went for the pencil skirt and not only did I feel pleasantly dressed, I was completely comfortable, with nothing digging in, pulling or tourniquet-ing my waist. I also felt a lot calmer than I used to after a session fighting an outfit together. In fact, I wasn't remotely close to tears at any time. Hallelujah.

What I find so terrifying is that such a small weight loss could make such a huge difference. I probably don't even look that different to anyone else, but inside me the shift is exponential. Of course I am thrilled to be less porky, but what breaks my heart is to think that I could have saved myself so much angst and aggro if only I had given up alcohol, sugar and simple carbohydrates years earlier.

But as a lifelong proselytiser against the fat fascists of the fashion world, it is also hard to accept that while I still passionately believe that any woman should have the right to feel good about herself whatever size or shape she is, I feel so much better the closer I get to the 'accepted' size.

I've seen all too many times the damage that eating disorders can do to women who get obsessed with the unachievable catwalk and celluloid image, and I rail against the value system that imposes it upon us. But while I still loudly protest against that impossible, ultra-thin child-woman 'ideal', I now realise that in condemning that, we shouldn't confuse it with a desire to be a healthy weight for your height.

Starving yourself to try and look like a genetically freakish supermodel is dangerous; eating moderately to stay your own ideal weight is not, and I think for a long time I allowed myself to confuse the two. Which was a very convenient mindset when approaching a large piece of orange cake.

In that spirit, I threw away my bathroom scales years ago in order not to be morbidly obsessed by weight. Now I've bought a new pair and I intend to use them once every week, to keep myself at a more comfortable poundage than the one I had crept up to in blissful ignorance of the truth.

And I have a specific reason I really can't afford to put on any weight – if I do, my new Chloé pants won't fit me.

Southbound breasts

I am beginning to think the early feminists were right about burning their bras. Mind you, there is a big debate these days about whether that historic event ever actually happened, although I'm sure I've seen file footage.

Whatever – I hope it did happen, as I've always rather related to it, although the concept quickly became such a cliché of the women's liberation movement that it took on the taint of the ridiculous and was often used to belittle the whole struggle. Still is. Which is probably why feminist academics are now disowning it.

'Ooh, one of those bra-burners are you?' was certainly a classic 'humorous' put-down when I started out in the workplace. I remember one particularly odious public school pig saying it to me when he noticed that all the books I had bought in the literary editor's annual book sale happened to be published by Virago, which only published works by women writers, many of them long-neglected masterpieces.

'Trying to make a statement, are we?' he sneered. 'Bit of

a bra-burner, are we?' No, actually, 'we' just happen to like Rosamund Lehman and Eudora Welty. Grrrrrr. It still rankles with me and it happened back in 1986. What a farthog.

Anyway, I've been thinking about the whole issue of bras and bosoms recently because in the past week I have come across two 'ground-breaking' new products concerning that area of the female anatomy.

'Nippits – The Perfect Solution' are 'sheer, featherlight, latex-free, adhesive nipple concealment strips that are totally effective in preventing visibility . . .' Not convinced? There's more: 'Unlike any other product, they do not cover the aureole and are padless, making a smooth *natural* look.'

Now, what exactly is natural about having no nipples? The only women I know who don't have any lost them to devastating and essential breast cancer surgery. Why would anyone want to buy pieces of sticky-backed plastic to hide their nipples? They should feel thrilled still to have them.

I know it can be a bit embarrassing if your headlights come on in a cold room among mixed company, but it shouldn't be. Nipples are simply part of a woman's body and it's only other people's attitudes to them that make them 'dirty', something that shouldn't be shown in public. Somehow it is all right these days to reveal practically the entire breast, but not the outline of an erect nipple. If you ask me, that's because a fat wedge of visible breast is a good perve for the onlooker, while hard nipples represent active female arousal, which is still taboo. But then, I would think that. I'm one of those bra-burners.

The other product I've recently been sent are stick-on strips to hold your breasts up, so you can go braless, but still maintain that perky silicon look. I'm not sure why these piss me off so much – apart from the thought of ripping them off your bare skin afterwards – but I think it's related to the same mindset that created killer corsets and bound feet. I'm just not comfortable (sorry) with the idea of physical distortion to be more 'attractive'. And don't even start me on breast enlargement surgery.

What we need to leave behind is the idea that bosoms without the perkiness of youth are somehow offensive. Southbound breasts are a fact of life and gravity, and the glorious office of motherhood, in particular, changes your boozies for ever. Tuppence in a long sock is the best description I've heard of the maternal breast, but does that mean I have to strap them up with gaffer tape?

As a casual glance at *National Geographic* will reveal, this is not something that bothers African tribeswomen. I don't know exactly what their stand is, but maybe a breast showing obvious signs of suckling is a source of pride to them. In our culture it seems to be a mark of shame.

And now I'm off to burn my Nippits.

All change

One of the worst aspects of being young in the 1970s was communal changing rooms. It seems hard to imagine now, in these days of Witchery's pale wood floors, designer fit-outs and helpful salespeople, but back then young fashion stores had one big room for everyone to try things on in.

Just girls, mind you, not pervy unisex – but believe me, it was vile enough. On a hot summer Saturday the communal fitting room of Miss Selfridge's London flagship store was as fetid as the Wallabies' change shed after an All Blacks clash – and I have it on good authority that the equivalents in Melbourne and Sydney were just as noisome. Honky-tonky in the extreme.

Not only were there other people's feet to cope with, there were other people's armpits and other people's underwear (or lack of it) to confront as well. Not to mention the bastards who were very interested in other people's handbags.

The constant threat of your hard-earned Saturday job money being liberated from your clutches meant that you had to keep one eye on how ugly, fat and foul you were looking in that denim jumpsuit, another on how good the tall, slim girl in the other corner was looking in the same thing, and another on your bag, which was not easy, as you can imagine.

Then there was all the bending, arm-lifting, huffing and grunting associated with trying on ill-made clothes that are slightly too small for you. And it was very disconcerting, lifting your head from a downward position to see straight up someone's bum.

In this regard the communal set-up was particularly interesting in jeans shops, with everybody lying twitching on the floor like half-dead flies, trying to zip them up. The next stage of the jeans-fitting process was the bending over to tuck under about three metres of excess denim, followed by Russian dancer bouncing crouches, to see whether it would ever be possible to sit down in them. It was like being accidentally caught onstage during a big production number in *Seven Brides for Seven Brothers*.

Another danger of communal fitting rooms was the scary gangs of rough girls shopping in packs. You seriously had to make sure one of them didn't catch you accidentally looking at her – 'What choo lookin' at?' – and if you had brought in something to try on that they fancied, like, say, an egg-yolk-yellow fun-fur bomber jacket, they'd have it off your peg and on their sweaty bodies in a minute, daring you to object. It was particularly interesting when they did this with something you already owned.

These terrifying types were just one of several reasons why you would never venture into those hellholes without your own posse of gal pals. Apart from needing a sounding-board for the obvious 'Do I look very fat in this?' questions (usually answered without your best friend taking her eyes off herself in the mirror), you needed protection and a bag-handler.

Woe betide the girl who shopped alone in those places, because if you'd brought the wrong size in, you had to get completely re-dressed and head back out into the dark and noisy melee of the shop floor – carrying all your stuff and all the garments you were still considering – to try to find the right one.

Plus you would lose your crucial corner pozzie, with two mirrors and two hooks, and might even have to endure the worst of tortures: the middle of the room try-on, with all your possessions scattered around on the floor like handbags at a disco, dodging fellow shoppers, while trying to get sight of yourself in a mirror.

Considering what I went through back then in the pursuit of fashion, it's a miracle I wasn't put off shopping for life. And probably a pity.

Trump tonsure

One of the most satisfactory trends to develop over recent years, in my opinion, is for men who are losing their hair just to plunge in and have the lot cropped off.

It is such a bold and positive statement that I always think says a lot about the chap in question. The kind of things it says are: I'm practical, I'm confident and I think I've got a nice-shaped head. I applaud those men.

Which is why I am sitting here in a state of shock looking at a picture of Donald Trump. I have been staring at it now – and the others in the same article about him, his lovely new wife and his lovely new money – for about ten minutes, because I just can't get over it.

Mr Trump is clearly losing his hair, but not for him a trip to the barber for a number two; oh no, he has opted instead for the comb-over. That most terrible of hair choices, far worse than the weave, or even the full-on wig. Even a glam-metal perm is a better look than a comb-over.

And it gets worse. Donnie's do is not even your normal

comb-over arrangement, with a special long piece of hair growing on one side of the head, which is pulled over and glued just above the other ear. It's a comb-*forward*. In fact, it starts so far down his neck, it could be back hair he's using. It's a shocker.

If he ever gets caught in a brisk wind – and it can fairly whistle down those Manhattan concrete canyons he so loves to build on – that mat of hair must fly up like a trapdoor. If gravity then deposits it where it belongs, at the back of his head, he must look like a heavy-metal roadie in a bespoke Brioni suit – which is the only brand he wears these days, according to this interview.

'I used to pride myself on buying very inexpensive suits,' says the Donster, something I find easy to believe, looking at these pictures.

'Over the years, I've learned that is wrong. These days I go for Brioni, whose service and attention to detail is second to none. The way we dress says a lot about us before we ever say a word.'

Too true, Trumpman, so please explain – how can someone who has enough savvy to appreciate the finest suits on earth possibly walk away from the mirror with his hair like that?

Because if, as according to his own theory, his suit is saying: 'I'm incredibly rich and discerning, too – I know top schmutter when I see it and only the best is good enough for Donnie Boy,' what on earth does he think his hair is saying?

Well, my first suggestion for that speech bubble competition was: 'I'm not middle-aged. And that's an order.' But thinking about it a little more, I started to wonder if it might not be something more along these lines: 'I'm not middle-aged. Please?'

But really I can't decide if walking around with such a blatant and unconvincing denial of the truth on his head is an act of supreme over-confidence, tragic insecurity, or just plain self-delusion.

I'm mostly inclined towards the latter, because the person that Trumpton's rug puts me instantly in mind of is Michael Jackson. It smacks of the same inability to see oneself clearly in the mirror.

There is an official medical condition in relation to people with eating disorders, called 'body image dysmorphia', describing what happens when a skeletal anorexic looks in a mirror and sees Fatty Bigbum looking back.

Trumpo clearly has an advanced case of rug dysmorphia. Maybe he sees himself as he was aged twenty-five smiling back, which must be lovely for him, but really, he does need to be told the truth.

So can someone please ask Elton John to call him with some useful numbers?

The young

I recently attended a very marvellous event at a house near where I live. The owners are generous people of artistic inclination and every once in a while, when the mood takes them, they throw open the doors to their sprawling lower floor and fill it with friends and friends of, for an evening of hearty food and live music (and quite a lot of wine). Just because they can, really.

The night I went, there were five female performers, a mixture of amateur and professional, with one once-well-known cabaret singer coming out of retirement to make us all hoot and roar; and another who sings like she is channelling Ella Fitzgerald, Billie Holiday and Janis Joplin simultaneously. Fabulous stuff.

Really, the whole thing was bliss, but apart from the generally life-affirming effect of live music and people who can be bothered, there was something else which made the evening quite magical. The hosts have children in their mid-twenties and they were there, along with a crowd of their friends.

They were so beautiful.

It was like having a flock of exotic birds or butterflies in the room, as they flitted around in wonderfully eccentric clothes they had mostly designed themselves. (The mother of the house had an iconic fashion label in the 1970s, so it is in their blood.)

And I wasn't the only one who noticed it. Several of my friends – we are all in our forties and beyond – also commented on it.

It wasn't that these young people were amazingly Gucci ad/Natalia Vodianova/Gemma Ward/film star beautiful. It was a more complex combination of above-average looks with innate style, an air of open-minded intelligence, and then the final ingredient: youth.

I don't think that ever before have I been so properly aware of the potency of fully ripened youth. I mean, it's not exactly a new idea; I understood the concept, but it wasn't until that night that I really appreciated its power.

I have seen gilded youth before en masse, in particular at Henley Regatta, possibly the greatest festival of erotica I have ever attended, in terms of beautiful young men at their peak. But back when I used to go to that event, I wasn't much older than those glorious rowers myself, so checked them out from a different point of view. They were gorgeous among my peer group.

Only now, however, from the perspective of proper middle age, having recently, I think, come to accept that all vestiges of my own youth are completely gone, could

I really appreciate the magic of youth.

It has an almost alchemical effect on the atmosphere in a room, I realised, spreading a sense of joy and celebration – even among those, like myself, who are looking back at it.

Just a couple of years ago, when I was still desperately clinging to the very last shreds of my own, I think the combined impact of their youthful radiance might have depressed me. I would have felt less-than, left out, left over. But the other night? I just felt joyous looking at them. And slightly relieved.

They say that youth is wasted on the young, but I can remember clearly the sense of responsibility I felt when I wore its mantle. The urgency always to look wonderful and to be having a spectacular time – to fulfil other people's expectations of what it should be like to be Young – frequently made me miserable.

Now I can enjoy other people's youth in a way that I couldn't always relish my own and I take great comfort in the knowledge that as each generation fades to grey, another will be coming up into bloom behind them.

Far from a cruel reminder of former glories, the eternal wellspring of youth is the greatest possible comfort to those of us who are looking forward only towards old age.

Junk sadness

I am obsessed with junk. Op shops, garage sales, flea markets, boot fairs – I love them to an almost unhealthy degree. I can get as excited by what I might find in a big old junk shed as I would in Barneys or Harvey Nichols. Mostly. But sometimes junk shopping makes me so sad, I have to run away and eat a cake.

It happened this morning. A friend texted me to say that she'd seen some old chintz curtains in a local emporium that she thought I would love. So I headed over there on a weekday morning and it left me feeling lower than the Mississippi delta.

Maybe it was because junketeering is normally a hard-earned weekend treat and on a Thursday morning I really should have been in my office working, so I felt guilty rather than excited from the outset.

There was also the location of the shop. It's in a poor part of town and while they style it as an 'antiques centre', really it's just a group of slightly desperate traders selling off the sorry detritus of other people's lives in a really sordid old shop. It smells of damp and old shoes.

Then there was the fact that the curtains weren't my thing at all. I could see why my friend thought I would like them – they were flowery – but I really didn't. So that added disappointment to guilt; a potent combo.

I should have just left then, but my tat addiction wouldn't let me. I had to poke around in every corner of that hellhole in case the perfect old jug, or lidless teapot, or embroidered pillowcase, or amateur painting or souvenir headscarf was hidden there, just waiting for me to rescue it. It wasn't. Although I did unearth some nice old nursery napkins for my household linen-obsessed best friend, who has a big birthday coming up.

But that find wasn't enough to stave off the junk sadness – especially as I knew I was paying slightly too much for them – and by the time I tore myself away from that godforsaken dive, I felt seriously low.

In the end it was the toys that really did it. Not just the sentimental idea of the determinedly cheerful old monkey with a jolly red fez on his head and stripy trousers that *nobody wants any more* – although there was one and it was pretty poignant. Poor old Bobo.

It was the collection of costume dolls from around the world that finally finished me off. I could so clearly see the little girl who used to own those dolls and the delight on her face every time Daddy brought her home a new one. It was so clearly a *collection*, once proudly displayed, and now it was just a heap in a box. I felt so lowered as I looked at them.

Then it was like the whole shop filled up with the ghosts of the children who had owned all the toys. I could see their little faces and feel their excitement at getting something new – and here it all was, reduced to dust and desolation.

Not that those children are necessarily dead now; they are probably living meaningful adult lives, but as the mother of a nearly four-year-old myself, any reminders of the fleeting nature of childhood become very unbearable.

Especially when your little angel is being looked after by someone else while you are supposed to be working, but actually you are wasting your life – and hers – in a foul junk shop.

I'm OK now. I'm in my office, I've had a bun, I've spoken to my daughter on the phone, and as the day has gone on I've become glad I had that intense junk shop tristesse, because it's taught me a lesson.

I won't go junketeering again until I feel I've earned it – and I'll take her with me. And if she wants that monkey, she can have him.

Food scares

The late Dr Atkins has finally finished me off in regard to food. Now I don't feel safe eating anything.

We've all been brainwashed into being terrified of fat for years. Cheese, butter, the nice crispy bits on a lamb chop, let alone a gorgeously creamy cheesecake, were the enemy. Thanks to my friend the wholefood guru, I have long known that it's the trans-fats in hydrogenated vegetable oils which are the absolute killers, but it's still hard to feel safe in relation to animal fats and one's waistline, isn't it? Especially if you have ever been on the Scarsdale Diet.

But now I am told that my old food pals of the F-Plan years, when I thought it was a terrific idea to have a large, plain wholemeal roll for lunch – no butter! – and a brick-sized baked potato – no butter! – with baked beans for dinner, are equally ruinous to one's figure. Along with the accompanying huge raw-vegetable salad – no dressing!

I never thought the day would come when I would feel frightened of a celery stick. Mind you, I was already wary if it wasn't organic. All kinds of salad – high water content – and particularly carrots (very prone to pests) are to be avoided if you can't get the naturally farmed versions, because of the high levels of pesticides and fertilisers used to grow them against all odds. Potatoes make your arthritis worse, and so do tomatoes.

So what does that leave?

Of course, dairy has long been off-limits, by order of the naturopath push, who maintain that it is a food suitable only for baby cows, an argument I have always found specious, but which generalised food superstition made me take on board anyway.

The same crowd warned me off anything containing yeasts, which include mushrooms and raisins, as well as the more obvious bread, wine, beer and dear old Vegemite.

I've never actually been told I've got a wheat allergy, but being around those people makes you think you probably do, so that's another thing for the no-no list.

They reckon we should all eat a lot of quinoa, an ancient grain enjoyed by the Aztecs, or some such. Just trying it was enough for me to add that to my list of excluded foods all on my own. See also carob, an unusually nasty substance, redolent of freeze-dried dog turds.

I was led to try that monstrous cack by a general fear of chocolate, brought on not only by its high levels of fat – and trans fats too if you eat the really cheap stuff – and death sugar, but also the dreaded caffeine in it. For the same reason, coffee is absolutely out and tea is under serious scrutiny.

Did I mention shellfish? Shocking seabed scavengers of deadly polluting poisons, apparently. And tuna. Too much mercury. Got turned off that while I was pregnant and haven't felt the same about it since. Smoked salmon? Don't make me laugh. Antibiotics, pesticides and all the nightmare chemicals of intensive farming swilling around in a cage in the sea. Don't go there. Any kind of fish, actually, unless you've caught it yourself in an Arctic icehole. I've heard horror stories about deep-sea trawlers packing your lovely, fresh, low-fat fish in antibiotics to bring it back to shore unrotted. It doesn't matter if they were true or not, they're lodged in my brain.

Along with the idea that, unless it was raised organically, chicken is pumped with foul farm-eceuticals and hormones – and had a horrid life too. Eggs are full of salmonella and fat. And while BSE may not be a problem with the Aussie herd, the whole idea of it has made me wary of meat anyway. Even without the fat issue.

And now, thanks to Dr Atkins, I no longer even have refuge in the brown rice and vegies of the Liver Cleansing Diet, because they are chock-full of horror carbs.

I am deeply suspicious of a diet that won't let me eat an organic rice cake, so I'm going on a revolutionary new one. I'm going to eat whatever I damn well like.

Just say yes

My best friend Jo once threatened to have a T-shirt printed with the slogan: 'I've seen every knob in London.' The joke was not a reference to her private life, but to her long quest to find the perfect door fittings – knobs – for her new kitchen.

This decorating crusade took her to all compass points in that sprawling shopopolis in search of the überknob. And where did she find it in the end?

Not in the ancient, cobweb-strewn warehouse in Shoreditch (east), the brushed-steel designer zone of Islington (north) or the twee yummy mummy establishments of Wandsworth Bridge Road (south-west), but in a shop just yards from her front door.

She must have walked past that place about fifty times en route to far-flung knob Shangri-las, but just assumed they couldn't possibly have what she needed – it couldn't possibly be that easy. But it was.

What my friend had discovered – the hard way – was the Just Do It school of home decorating.

I discovered it myself recently by a simpler route. I had a plumber booked to put in my new shower on 5 January, which gave me a very limited time frame in which to order all the parts for it before the world shut down for two weeks on 24 December.

So, time-poor, with a small child and a large book deadline to juggle, I had no choice but to adopt a severely pragmatic approach to assemble the components. Ergo, I chose my tiles in approximately seven minutes, in the first and only tile shop I went to.

And that is another key rule of Just Do It Decorating: don't dismiss the first shop.

This is quite hard to take on for someone used to visiting, say, fifteen shoe emporia in pursuit of the perfect little flat sandal. But what you come to realise is that with interiors products, the choices available can be even greater than they are with fashion – which is saying something – and that the differences between items can be quite exquisitely subtle. So you have to decide just how much you are prepared to do your head in to achieve the effect you want.

I seriously brained myself earlier this year looking for fabric to reupholster some junk-shop Louis Fooey chairs. My mistake was going to the soft furnishings department of Liberty & Co, in London, which houses what must be the fabric swatch equivalent of the Alexandria Library. I left that repository of all things opulent and glorious a gibbering loon. There was just too much to choose from. The chairs still aren't covered.

So when it came to the shower, I was tough on myself. I chose the tiles from the first shop, as described, and then for the actual shower fitting I asked my knobs friend which taps company she recommended (she'd done a similar research job in that area when doing up her bathroom) and just ordered from them. I didn't even look at anything else.

I had a slight wobble over the shower door. Who knew there was a whole galaxy of shower-door companies out there? But in the end I was swayed by the 30 per cent discount off one which looked fine enough – and which the shop had in stock. Likewise, the shower tray involved driving around local plumbers' merchants for a morning, until I found one that was good enough, without having to order it from Sweden. The result is a sprauncy new shower which I totally love and which didn't cost me weeks of brain-ache.

So this is what I have learned: when making home improvements, the financial cost and stress of having tradesmen in the house is enough to deal with. You don't have to settle for tawdry 'it'll do' items, but you don't need to torture yourself over a tap, either.

And I mean that with knobs on.

Plastic fantastic

I had a moment of insight into the true depth of maternal love when I realised it had made me allow the foul pieces of plastic called My Little Ponies invade my generally tasteful home. They are bloody everywhere. But I have committed a much greater sin against taste for the occasion of my daughter's fourth birthday.

My original gift for her was a triumph of muted sensibilities. It is a vintage doll's cot – complete with drop side – which I found at a garage sale.

The nice old chap I bought it from said it was at least seventy years old, but I didn't really care – I was already in love with its faded duck-egg-blue paint, just worn and chipped enough. And the fact that Cath Kidston would probably fight me to the death over it. I spirited it immediately to a friend who is an amazing seamstress and commissioned her to make bedding for it out of fabulous old pieces of vintage fabric.

The result is unutterably divine. For me. That's what

I had to face up to when I got it down from the attic a few days before her birthday to wrap. The whole thing was really for me. Sure, it would look gorgeous in a magazine shoot of my home, but would my daughter like it? No!

She doesn't even relate to baby dolls particularly. The dolls she likes are Barbies, particularly Barbie Mermaidia with her lurid hair extensions, piercings and body art.

So I put the cot back in the attic and set out for the shops, where I bought my little girl an entire Disney Princess birthday.

She's getting a pop-up princess play castle; a Sleeping Beauty outfit, complete with tiara, necklace, shoes etc; and a Snow White doll (with her Woodland Friends). And I have wrapped it all in Disney Princess paper, with matching gift tags and birthday card. The big day isn't until next week, but I am confident this sorry bundle of plastics and polyester will elicit the sharp intake of breath every parent hopes to hear when their child opens a birthday present.

So why do I feel I have let her down in some way? I think it's because I feel fundamentally uncomfortable with the entire Disney oeuvre and deeply regret exposing her to it from a very young age. The first logo she ever recognised was the Mickey Mouse ears. I could have sobbed.

The reason I let her watch the films in the first place was because I remembered loving *101 Dalmatians* so very much as a little girl. I still love it – the 1950s drawings, the cute dogs, the campness; what I had forgotten was how violent it is. It was only when my little tot, then just two, started shouting 'Idiot!' at people that I realised.

I now see that the entire Disney canon contains either extreme violence or cruelty and that the bad people are usually post-menopausal older women: the wicked stepmother in *Snow White*, ditto in *Cinderella*, the wicked fairy in *Sleeping Beauty*, Madame Methuselah in *The Rescuers*, Ursula the Sea Witch in *The Little Mermaid* . . . I could go on.

There is usually terrible fighting, the heroine is always – but always – in serious jeopardy and conflict is always resolved by someone dying a violent death. The more of the films I have seen, the more the general atmosphere of hysterical paranoia, fear of difference and over-aggressive response reminds me of American foreign policy.

Consider instead, three of my favourite children's TV shows: *The Wiggles*, *The Koala Brothers* and *Charlie and Lola*. The first lot spend their time singing, dancing, having parties, eating ('Fruit salad, yummy yummy . . .') and having fun with multi-species friends. The second crew sort out small problems in the community. The latter work through issues of sibling tension, boundaries and acceptable behaviour. All of them do it with style, verve and humour.

So why is it the po-faced plastic princesses which all little girls seem to dote on?

One-track mind

I have been aware for a while of a behavioural tic that I have developed as a result of so many years' exposure to high fashion – a tendency to comment automatically on details of people's attire. It can be a remark about what someone is wearing on television, or it could be straight to their face.

Now, this is fine when you're at a wedding and you say to a friend 'I love your hat', or you're watching a movie and you whisper to your friend 'Isn't that leather gladiator kilt a great look on a man?'

It's just not so great when it becomes your primary mode of communication, so that whereas, in a slightly awkward social moment, most people would probably say, 'Hasn't it been hot?' I would tend to ask, 'Are those Notify jeans?'

It was my friend Wendy – a stand-up comedian – who nailed it for me, after I allowed it to tip over from the slightly eccentric to the seriously inappropriate. It was the day after I had been to see her husband's new stage show. He's a brilliant exponent of character comedy and his latest production is a series of monologues from seven characters. I was gushingly telling Wendy how much I had loved it, when out it popped: 'I just had one little problem,' my head heard my mouth saying, apparently on autopilot.

'It was that first character – you know, the disappointed solicitor who has become best friends with his drug-dealer clients? – I thought his clothes were wrong. The blazer was too tight and it was clearly polyester and it really put me off and made me think he was some kind of travelling salesman type. I think he needs to reconsider that look.'

I was so mortified after I put the phone down that I had to ring back and apologise. Who was I to make comments on Steve's show? He doesn't need my fashionista perspective on the production. Even while I was watching the show and obsessing on the jacket, I'd promised myself not to say anything about it, but then out it came, all on its own. It seemed completely involuntary.

Wendy was charming about it, but the next time I saw her, we were watching Live 8 together and I gradually became aware that my first comment on every act was about what they were wearing.

'Look at that dress!' I cheeped, as Mariah Carey waddled on. 'She looks like Miss Piggy at a Halloween party.'

'I can see why Kate Moss loves Pete Doherty – he can really carry off a drainpipe jean.'

'David Beckham's jeans are way too baggy.'

'Velvet Revolver define rock style.'

Yadda yadda yadda. I just couldn't stop, and I realised

I had hit a low point towards the end of the show. 'I wonder why Roger Waters wears his jeans belted so high?' my fashionista tongue was asking the room, as Pink Floyd played one of the most extraordinary sets of live music I have ever heard. 'He's still a handsome man but that look really ages him.'

I turned to Wendy.

'I've got a problem, haven't I?' I said. 'I can't judge anything in terms other than what people are wearing.'

'It's OK, Maggie,' said Wendy. 'You've just got Fashion Tourette's.'

She's right. And like the sufferers of that awful affliction, I really can't help myself. Which is fine when you are in a room of fashionistas, as I so often am, but really not on when you are with civilians.

But I felt better about it later, when our friend Hilary turned up to watch with us. Hilary styles interiors for magazine shoots. 'Oh look,' she said, as the coverage crossed to Jonathan Ross in a lavishly decorated interview room. 'It's all Designer's Guild . . .'

Clothes horse power

Proust had his madeleines and that wretched bloody doorknob which I have never been able to get past in *À la Recherche du . . . zzzzz*. I had my red wellington boots, my red raincoat and my red sou'wester. One whiff of a certain kind of PVC and I can completely recall the delicious plastic smell of that raincoat and the crackly sound it made when I moved. I can remember what the hat felt like (a bit scratchy round the forehead) and the plastic ties under the chin (sticky against the skin and always in the wrong place). Smell that kind of soft plastic and I have the total physical sensation of being rather hot and of socks coming astray inside wellingtons, the rubber a bit abrasive against fat little legs.

I can also remember the feeling of finding life a bit bewildering, but knowing that Mummy and bread and jam were safe bets and brothers were dangerous. I was three.

That ensemble is my first fashion memory. What seared it on my mind was that my big sister, seven years older, worship worship, had a larger version of the same outfit. I had something the same as her!

The first day it rained, she took me on an expedition in the garden, jumping into puddles, standing under drips, luxuriating in the thrill of being dry in the wet, until I ruined it by getting rather a lot of water inside my wellies and had to be taken inside.

But while it lasted, it was a lot of attention from a ten-year-old to a pesky three-year-old (who was more used to being left out of games) and I knew straightaway it was the outfit that had got it for me.

The next key garment I can remember was the psychedelic-print, flared hipster pants from Stafford's premier department store in 1967. I spotted them first. They were so groovy. They looked like something Micky Dolenz would wear and I had to have them. Then I told my best friend about the pants – and her mother bought them for her! I was so furious I picked on her for a week at school, leaving her out of games (I knew exactly how to do that) and telling her that I thought pink and yellow and green and turquoise (my favourite colour) looked hideous together.

Then I went home and drew pictures of the trousers obsessively and was so miserable that in the end my mother gave in and bought them for me. Everything was sweet again in the playground at St Dominic's. That was how I found out that liking the same clothes confirms friendships.

Then I discovered the fashion page in *The Sunday Times*. Oh, sweet revelation! Every week there were pictures of clothes and interesting things written about them. I devoured every word, thrilled there were people who said things like: 'When I find something I like, I buy it in several colours' and 'Una loves to pick up interesting pieces of clothing on film shoots in Morocco and Kashmir, and wears lingerie from her grandmother's trousseau.'

One week they did an article about a boutique especially for swinging kids on the Kings Road, Chelsea. It was called Kids in Gear. I had to have the exact outfit in the picture. More hipster flares, a body shirt with a large collar, an Indian waistcoat embroidered with mirrors, and a stetson. I cut the picture out and looked at it every day until my ninth birthday came around and we went to London to get my outfit.

Out I came, resplendent in a lime-green shirt, chocolate-brown elephant-cord pants and my waistcoat. I wore it to an Italian restaurant that night and when I couldn't choose between three puddings the waiter chucked me on the cheek and brought me all of them with a big wink.

That was how I discovered that having groovy clothes gets you all kinds of good stuff. I still can't decide whether that was a good thing to learn.

Hideous kinky

Sometimes I like trying clothes on just to see how hideous they will look on me. It's not some kind of self-esteem-destroying masochist's game – I just find it very amusing.

There is also something very interesting to me about the way that the clothes of some designers will just never suit one. Most shops and labels will yield something which flatters, but then there are these others which are just non-starters.

I can pretty much tell, when I am watching them go by on the catwalk, which outfits – however gorgeous – would make me look like a pregnant rhino. But I like trying them on in real life, as well, when possible, so I can: a) prove it to myself, and b) try and analyse what it is about them that is so wrong for me.

I had the perfect opportunity to undertake one of these missions the last time I was in Milan for the shows, at a small warehouse on the edge of town, which houses one of the greatest attractions of visiting that city for, I think, the majority of the female delegates. It's the Marni outlet.

I can hardly begin to describe the place that the label Marni holds in the heart of the average fashionista. It is adored with an almost religious fervour, a fetish really, beyond even the collective lust we feel for Prada ready-to-wear.

Prada clothes are impeccable, in my opinion, but Marni has a very specific appeal: it's less well known to the general public, it's not on sale in that many places around the world – and it's fantastically expensive.

Even beyond all these layers of exclusivity, it is also a little obscure in its colours and shapes. You have to have a very refined aesthetic to 'get' Marni. It has no sex appeal whatsoever, in the generally understood manner and – unless you know what it is – it doesn't even look expensive.

The final appeal of Marni, to those who subscribe to the cult, is that it only suits tall, slender, small-breasted women – and, in my opinion, only brunettes. Preferably ones who are married to architects or famous artists. They look absolutely wonderful in it – and I love the clothes – but as a short, chubby blonde (married to a retired footballer), I look hilarious in Marni.

It's not just that I'm too squat for it, or even that the 1950s-style jackets with their cropped, bracelet-length sleeves and shawl collars, in fabrics like leftovers from a Polish car seat factory, make me look frumpy. I just look mad in it. Mustard never has been my shade.

So I had a hilarious couple of hours in that warehouse with my fashion bestie, Mark, who was on the hunt for presents for his female workmates. I'd told him all the way there how bad I look in Marni and he wouldn't have it, but after I'd modelled a couple of shapeless duster coats in old rose tones, he fully believed me.

He believed me so much that he kept finding new things for me to try on, for our greater amusement. A very full skirt, gathered on to a waistband, will always make me look like a tea cosy, but a cropped kimono jacket in stiff, putty-coloured brocade was the high point.

The wide sleeves and slope shoulders, the washed-out colour and shiny fabric, were simply appalling on someone with broad shoulders, noticeable breasts, short arms and fair skin — and we were almost helpless with laughter.

By this point, people were giving us funny looks. We were laughing in the temple of Marni, where all the other women present were experiencing the racing pulse I would have at a 99 per cent off sale of Bottega Veneta tote bags.

But in my way, I was as happy as they were, leaving with six huge carrier bags of stuff each (true — I saw them). They'd had a shopping coup and I'd had a bloody good laugh.

Boot scooting

Question: of the many, many pairs of shoes, boots, sandals, sandshoes, mules, slippers and flippers that have graced my feet over the years, which do you think would be my most comfortable footwear of all time? The Havaiana thongs? The battered Nike neoprene trainers? Well-worn Birkenstocks? Cork-soled felted-wool orthopaedic clogs (they are certainly ugly enough to want to be comfy)? None of the above. The outright winners of this award are my battered black cowboy boots. No contest.

I've had them good ol' boys over twenty years now and they just keep getting better 'n' better (I just wish writing about them didn't make me mentally talk like George Bush, all you folks).

I can walk for hours in my cowbies and they never rub or pinch, or make my feet feel tired. They also have some mysterious property that makes it possible to wear them even on quite warm days without overheating, and of course they are beyond brilliant when it's cool. I like something I can slip on over a sock. Very comforting thing, a sock.

True, they're not quite so great in the wet, with the leather soles and all, which are getting thinner as the years and the kilometres of concrete go by, but I feel so happy whenever I wear my cowboy boots, I don't really mind if my toes get a bit damp.

There's just something about a boot, isn't there? Somehow you have a relationship with your boots that you don't have with any other footwear. There's a sense of a bond, of being in it together, of knowing that your boots will never let you down. Boots aren't mere accessories, they're mates.

As befits best mates, I can take my cowbies anywhere. They always fit in. They're great mixers, too. You can wear them with anything and I have. They look just as good with long skirts as they do with pants – better, really – and in my golden-thighed youth, I used to love wearing them with cut-off jeans and even miniskirts (but always with a big sweatshirt on top to avoid that trailer trash look).

They may not have the postmodern ironic flirtatiousness of a Prada mule, the chic of a Chanel pump, or the pure sex appeal of a Manolo stiletto, but I always have an extra spring in my step when I climb into those boots. They make me feel cool and ageless, like some kind of junior Georgia O'Keeffe type of person. Or Sheryl Crow's rather chubby older sister.

Even though they have been worn for decades by all kinds of respectable people who have never been anywhere near a rodeo, cowboy boots are still slightly outsider wear. To wear them is to say: I go my own way (and I'm sure Stevie Nicks has quite a collection of them herself, to work back with a wafty frock and a bit of a macramé skullcap).

It's no wonder they've always been a staple of the rock 'n' roll wardrobe. Real rockers always wear boots, rather than shoes, and cowbies have that requisite rock style detail – like jeans and leather pants – of looking better the older and more worn-in they get. And, of course, they are simply genius to dance in.

Cowboy boots are also a tribal marking. Not so niche as Marilyn Manson make-up, an Hermès Birkin bag, or a skin-head number one crop, but nevertheless an indication that the inhabitant thereof is not likely to be your average square peg. (Unless you are in Texas, when all such bets are off.)

The only thing that has got weird for me is that, after twenty years of wearing them with no regard whatsoever for prevailing trends, suddenly cowboy boots are ultra-fashionable among the young and cool creative crowd. I've been stopped on the street by girls with terrifying haircuts asking me where I bought my boots.

'You can't buy boots like these,' I want to say. 'You have to earn them.'

Gloves off

It was all about gloves. According to the fashion shows that had just finished in Europe, the glove was the key new item we would all need to update our wardrobes for next winter. Hurrah.

Not just any old gloves, mind, but some *feature* gloves in a witty colour – new-leaf-green would be ideal, especially if they were ostrich skin. And preferably they should be long gauntlets which would stretch up to the elbow if allowed, but are worn scrooched down to the wrist in artless folds. That was the important differential from the last time the feature glove was the go, back in the 1980s, when it was a short glove you wanted and, ideally, red. Mine were and I did love them so.

The first time I saw the New Glove (at the Prada show in Milan), I could have clapped my (gloveless) hands in delight, because it looked so right and I thought it so clever of them to come up with a new accessory necessity, now that we all have more handbags and belts than we know what to do with. And one which, like the shoe and the handbag, does not present any possible humiliations of a sizing nature, which was a drawback with some of those belts that were meant to sit insouciantly on the hip, but sometimes tourniqueted the waist when tried on in public in a pretentious boutique.

Then, in the midst of all this excitement about forthcoming shopportunities, I made a few discoveries about the new It accessory. There is a bit more to gloves than I initially thought.

I had the first revelation at a cocktail party in Paris where I was chatting to my very chic friend Joan Burstein, founder of legendary London fashion emporium Browns, who has been elegant for much longer than I have been alive. She was with a friend of equal style and vintage. I was enthusing about the new glove, and Joan's friend – who was not only elegant, but also *une vraie Parisienne* – said: 'In our day you simply did not leave the house without gloves and a hat. It was unthinkable.'

Joan agreed and lifted up the short fur jacket (purple-dyed chinchilla) she had resting over her right arm and showed me that she was holding a pair of exquisite black gloves trimmed with white piping. It was the way she was holding them that struck me. The palms were together, the fingers were smooth and she was grasping them lightly by their cuffs.

Her friend laughed and lifted the pashmina she had folded over her arm to reveal another pair of beautiful gloves in an identical arrangement. (She was holding a pair of spectacles very delicately by their arms too, and a glass of champagne. Reckon she could join the Peking Circus.)

I showed them my gloves. They came out of my coat pockets like a pair of mummified rat remains. All curled up and a bit crispy. They were good gloves, too, once. Black kid.

The next thing I learned about gloves was from an extract in American *Vogue* from Andre Leon Talley's recently published memoir. It was the most moving tribute to his grandmother, who brought him up, and it described how she had never allowed a shortage of money to compromise her innate sense of elegance.

'Mama' as he called her, never went out without gloves – and she always carried a spare pair in her handbag in case the first pair got dirty. Later in life, Mr Talley read that the Duchess of Windsor lived by the same rule.

So far from being some easy-option instant outfit update, it seems gloves demand a certain amount of savoir faire. But I'm optimistic. I did get past the need for the piece of elastic through my coat sleeves, so perhaps one day I will also learn how to hold my gloves like a lady. Perhaps.

Ginger nuts

I have recently read three really good novels – *Don't You Want Me?* by the brilliantly funny India Knight, *Shagpile* by my pal Imogen Edwards-Jones and *Atonement* by Mr Literary Smartypants himself, Ian McEwan.

One thing united these very different reads – they all show the most appalling discrimination against redheads. India Knight uses the fact that the male romantic lead has red hair as the pivot of her entire plot – her (hilarious and wonderful) main character Estella de la Croix cannot possibly fancy her otherwise perfect and hunky artist lodger Frank, because he's a carrot top.

Imogen Edwards-Jones uses the crime of ginger hair to further demonise the fabulously appalling coarse and lecherous husband of her lead character Madeleine. (She also describes him tucking his emerald-green dinner shirt into his red Y-fronts, to very amusing effect – the book is set in 1976.)

Now, those two are funny, wicked babe writers, known for being unafraid of an outrageous remark, but I was shocked at

Ian McEwan. I'm sure it was all part of the incredibly clever and carefully contrived set-up of the book (and it does set you right up, let me tell you, if you haven't read it), but there on page nine we come across the first bit of gingerism.

The three rather unfortunate children ('refugees from a bitter domestic civil war') who come to stay with the Tallis family are immediately set out as being less-than in the eyes of ghastly, precocious Briony Tallis (whom we are, of course, meant to hate), because 'all three were ginger-haired and freckled'.

OK, I understand that the riff about how the fairytale characters of young Briony's play, which she wants them to perform, could never be freckled, is a device to show us what a nasty little girl she is, but it still annoyed me. Can someone please tell me: What is wrong with red hair and freckles?

I love red hair – all shades from the most carroty orange to strawberry blonde and dark auburn – and I think freckles are really attractive too, so why do people go on about it so?

If, for example, I read one more nasty reference to the Simply Red singer Mick Hucknall and his red hair I am going to found an Anti-Gingerism League and have protest marches. I hate his pappy music as much as the next person, but you can't blame it on his hair colour.

Now, I have to admit I have, over the years, made a few unkind remarks about reddish hair myself, but it has always been with regard to people adopting red hair who don't have it naturally. Elton John and Paul McCartney in particular.

. And that is the really weird thing about this irrational anti-ginger movement – for every beautiful natural red-head forced to experience this cruel discrimination, there is someone else paying a fortune to go red at the hairdressers.

I can see why – some of the most attractive people I have ever known have been redheads. There is such a wonderful exoticism about madly red hair, especially when combined with that wonderfully fine-textured, creamy skin which often seems to go with it. Yet time and again I read nasty comments about it. If you said such things about black people or albinos there would be public outrage.

I mean, just try substituting the idea of 'black' for 'ginger' in any of the books described above. If Ian McEwan had used 'all three were black with Afro hair' instead of 'ginger-haired and freckled', he would have been vilified, not shortlisted for the Booker Prize. I'm beginning to wonder if gingerism hasn't become some kind of outlet for basic human bigotry in our increasingly politically correct society.

In the mean time I've got four words for unrepentant gingerists: Ann-Margret, Peter O'Toole.

Heels of steel

I've come up with a new sporting event that would be perfect for the 2012 London Olympics: Women's Competitive High Heel Wearing.

For reasons I am still trying to understand, getting around in ridiculously vertiginous high heels has become a status symbol among women of a certain ilk. Not just at cocktail parties, but for daywear. For *work*.

Just yesterday I was at a standing-room-only fashion event at which the PR was wearing Gucci heels so high that most women would only be able to lie down in them. It was 3 pm and I wanted to lie down just looking at her.

When I first noticed this syndrome, I thought it was some kind of statement along the lines of: the higher the heels you can cope with, the more of a woman you are, in a sex goddess kind of a way.

Wearing what amounted to fetish heels for daywear seemed akin to strapping yourself into stockings and suspenders (yuck) out of choice when there are perfectly good tights available. But I've subsequently realised that competition heels are not really about sex at all. They're not aimed at men – they're aimed at other women. It's a power thing.

Speaking of power, American *Vogue* editor-in-chief Anna Wintour, who basically runs world fashion, is famous for only wearing high heels. Manolo Blahnik high heels, to be precise. As she says in her foreword to his book *Manolo Blahnik: Drawings*: 'The truth is, I wear no other shoes but his.'

So I was interested to read a 'Me and My Overpriced Wardrobe' type article featuring the editor of the recently launched *Teen Vogue*, Amy Astley, in which she smugly confides: 'I only ever wear Manolo Blahnik heels.'

What a Mini-Me – and how interesting that she has chosen that particular aspect of Wintour's persona to imitate. It strikes me as distinctly *All About Amy*. She seems to be declaring that, like Wintour, she's tough enough to work a sixteen-hour day in tottering power heels, without ever resorting to the tragic barefoot-in-the-art-department look I used to be guilty of back in my magazine editor days, if I was ever stupid enough to wear heels into the office. That kind of physical endurance takes serious iron lady discipline – and funnily enough, Margaret Thatcher always wore high heels while she was in power.

But it was in Amy and Anna's milieu, at the European fashion shows, that the concept of high-heel competitiveness first struck me. In that context, wearing inappropriate party shoes before lunch is a neon sign declaring that you work on a high-status, big-budget magazine and are ferried from show to show in a chauffeur-driven limo.

You simply can't walk Milan's cobbled streets, or the long corridors of the Paris Metro, as more lowly delegates like me needs must, in ten-centimetre stiletto salon shoes. So the glamour girls at the shows in heels look down on we drones in flats, both metaphorically and literally.

I put on some heels myself (nine centimetres) a minute ago to remind myself what that sense of superiority is all about. I did feel instantly more elegant, taller, more in charge. There is no doubt that heels have transformative qualities, which can be great when you use them to boost your own self-esteem. It's just the element of using them to undermine other women's I don't like.

It's similar to the air of superiority some women adopt when they contrive to eat less than all the other chicks at the lunch table, and it makes me feel almost as uncomfortable as wearing high heels all day.

But there is hope. I saw that fashion PR again yesterday after she thought everyone had gone. I popped back up to get something and there she was – wearing her Birkenstocks.

Handbag black holes

Notice to all purveyors of accessories: I am never, not ever, buying another handbag unless I'm allowed to take it out for a test drive first.

I'm not speaking here of the little fun bags that you buy for parties, or summer hols, but your investment type of working handbag, racking up at over the crucial $500 mark, which is all too easy to pass these days.

When you're spending that kind of money you really do need the test drive, because it doesn't matter how schooled you are in the art of handbag-choosing – and I've had quite a bit of experience – you really can't tell, until you've spent a day with it, walking around the city, trying to get things done, whether it's a wonderbag, or just the weight of the world upon your shoulders.

It's one of many things I might understand better had I been less poleaxed by boredom during double physics at school, but some bags which feel quite light when empty become lead weights when you pop your wallet, keys, comb, lippie, mobile, Palm Pilot, several paper clips, a leaky ballpoint, three mystery business cards (who? where? why?), one boiled lolly and a newspaper into them.

Others, which feel similar in weight empty, seem to distribute the gravitorial drag of the same contents in a way that just lightly kisses your shoulder as you stroll along, window-shopping. Tra la la. How?

The other thing you can't predict very precisely, until you're out there with it, is a bag's rootle quotient. This is the amount of time it takes you to find your wallet/keys/ ringing phone among all the other detritus therein, without tipping the whole lot out on to the pavement.

Rare is the woman who buys more than one bucket bag in the same lifetime – they are the black holes of the handbag universe. But even those knicky-knacky bags which have handy separated pockets for the efficient filing of personal effects can become black holes for your wallet, while a grumpy taxi-driver waits to be paid.

Some work brilliantly, enabling you to find and answer your mobile without even looking, while others seem to swallow possessions up like quicksand, and I've never found a way of predicting which will be which.

I am speaking of all this from recent and bitter experience. Today was the maiden voyage of my latest investment handbag, and I had to put it on the ground to rootle for my wallet this morning, in exactly the taxi scenario described above. I do not care for *crouching*, in tailored clothing, on a busy city street, and I was not a happy girl. He was not a happy taxi-driver.

Plus, I realised, as he drove off in snarls of exhaust fumes, the bag doesn't have those protective little metal feet and in my confusion I had put it down in a damp, dirty gutter. It's bright orange canvas – now murky on the underside – and will never be the same.

Not only that, it also failed the load-bearing test, becoming impossibly heavy and awkward when I put my newspaper in it. Or, rather, crammed it in. What had seemed to be a perfect media pocket on the back of this enervating object turned out to be big enough only for a copy of *Reader's Digest*.

And that wasn't the end of it. In the shop, the handles had seemed to have that all-important quality of being just long enough to sit nicely on the shoulder, while also short enough to hold comfortably in the hand.

Out in the field, I found it kept slipping off my shoulder and made me feel like a long-armed baboon when held the hand way. So I spent the day like Margaret Thatcher with the thing looped over the crook of my arm, which is a very frumpifying look and not at all convenient for going through train turnstiles.

I can't take it back – it's got gutter stains on it – so I'm stuck with it. Next time, I'm insisting on a road test.

Family favourites

We were like three sailors on shore leave: my mum, my sister and me, let loose in a really nice clothes shop together. And most importantly, it was just us, with no-one else waiting grumpily outside, or running around pulling all the carefully folded sweaters off the shelves, or wanting to go to the playground, or the pub, or just home, anywhere but a *shop*.

It was utter bliss. We've shopped together more recently in all the possible variations of pairs, but I don't know the last time the three of us have done it together – it could have been Biba, it was so long ago. But it was quickly apparent that despite the long break and a combined age of 180 years, none of us had lost our zeal for it. And being reunited in our favourite activity after so long made us almost giddy with excitement.

Without even having to discuss it, we commandeered a row of changing rooms and between us we must have tried on everything in the shop, which had just the right balance of tasty items of good quality with non-silly price tags.

There was a great swapping of items between cubicles – 'can I try on that peacock-blue floral satin skirt when you've finished with it?' – plus much parading of potential combinations, and regarding of self in another's mirror, which somehow always seems better than the one in your own changing room.

We all quickly got into that state of retail euphoria in which, secure that there was always someone on handbag-monitoring duty, we felt free to wander the shop semi-clad, fossicking for ever-more enticing items. Really, we were like a pack of she-wolves bringing rodents back to our cave.

Adding to the general heaven of it – apart from a shared understanding that we all place an equal value on the place of clothing in the scheme of our lives (high) – was the very unusual benefit of knowing that when you asked one of the others for her honest opinion, you would actually get it.

Even with the best of girlfriends, you know she still always has one eye on herself in the mirror as she assesses your look. But when shopping *en famille*, there is pack pride at stake. I wasn't going to let anyone in my pack wear that peacock-blue floral skirt, for example. The colours were way too Miami for our collective colouring.

Equally, when I asked my sister to help me choose between the five dark brown cardigans I was auditioning, I knew I was getting a truly honest appraisal.

'I like the feature detailing on that one,' she said, regarding me with full concentration, 'but the shorter length makes you look a bit square.' Out it went.

My mother was equally blunt in her comments. I was suffering badly from *Kath 'n' Kim* muffin top syndrome that day, with my overtight jeans poojing all my midriff squashy bits up over the low waistband.

'I feel like I've got a rubber ring round my middle,' I said, regarding the resulting bulges inside yet another brown cardie in her cubicle mirror.

'You have,' she said, cheerfully, later commenting, in what was meant to be a positive rating on a heavier weight, dark brown cardigan: 'You look quite slim from the back.'

Finally, as we stood at the counter, marshalling our choices – a pair of navy pants for my sister, two long-sleeve, button-neck tops (one brown, one khaki) for my mum, and – guess what? – a dark brown cardie for me, my mother looked thoughtful.

'Why do you think we all love shopping so much?' she asked.

'Because we all live in places where there aren't any nice shops?' I suggested.

There was a pause.

'How did *that* happen?' said my sister, and we all fell about laughing.

Acting your age

Here are several reasons to be cheerful.

A UK-based Scottish actress friend of mine is currently up for the lead role in a major new American TV series. It's a huge deal and I really hope she gets it (maybe she'll take me to the Golden Globes as her date, yahoo! Better start doing some sit-ups to get into my dress), but it's also quite extraordinary.

Not that my mate wouldn't be great for the part – she's a brilliant actress, beautiful and hilarious – but I was mystified as to why they were considering a Scottish person to play an American woman in an American production that is going to be filmed in Los Angeles.

Of course, I had to find a tactful way to ask her that.

'Why don't they get an American actress?' I heard my mouth saying, while my brain was still mulling it over.

'Because they're all so Botoxed they can't show the range of emotion necessary for the part,' she replied.

Wow – that thrilled me. The first sign that the tide is

turning against plastic fantastic beauty. And then the very next day after I heard that, the equally un-botoxed, non-liposucked, un-face-lifted Helen Mirren won the Oscar for Best Actress.

It wasn't so much that she won the award – it's well chronicled that actors generally have a better chance at that gong playing a role seriously at odds with their reality: disabled, bonkers, barely human, anciently old etc. And you can't get much weirder than the British royal family, so while her performance was extraordinary, it was a great Academy Award role as well.

What was thrilling – and important – about the whole event, in my opinion, was how she looked on the night: bloody gorgeous. She's sixty-two. She claims she hasn't had any surgery. And she wasn't gorgeous in a patronising 'good for her age' mother-of-the-bride kind of way, either; she just looked fabulous, all other details irrelevant.

Now, of course, Helen Mirren has always been ridiculously beautiful – and famously sexy. In fact, I used to find her quite annoying, the way people were always going on about it. Any interview you read with her, you could practically see the reporter's drool on the page. And then there was that relationship with the young Liam Neeson, of course, which I still find it quite hard to forgive her for (please join me in a rousing chorus of 'It should have been me').

But I think I can get over it now, on account of the role model she has become for young actresses – and women in general. And men too, come to think of it. Any way you look at it, beautiful Helen Mirren, her face cross-hatched by quite deep lines, is a win-win for all of us.

So if she's not having surgery or paralysing injections, or even colouring her hair, what is she doing to hold on to that beauty and to that legendary sex appeal, so far past the age when it is supposed to be possible for women? I've done some research and she doesn't have a personal trainer – she claims to get her exercise walking her dogs – and I can't find any interviews espousing cranky diet regimes or hothouse yoga.

Studying the pictures, I reckon she is fortunate to have been born with a very warm skin tone and a naturally defined waist. The key things she is adding to these attributes at this stage is the steely grey hair – so much more flattering than a desperation dye job – and wonderful posture. I think the posture is a large part of it, so we'd all better do some Alexander Technique quick smart.

But most of all, I think it is her attitude to ageing – which was clearly ingrained in her from childhood. She quotes her own mother telling her this: 'Don't worry about getting older; nature has a wonderful way of maturing your mental faculties so that you don't mind the physical side of ageing.'

Young actresses everywhere, listen up.

You couldn't make it up

Here's a question: Who won the Oscar last year for Best Hair? And for Best Make-up? (And I mean in an actual film, not on the red carpet.) Bet you don't know – I certainly don't, or for any other year for that matter, which is wrong, because the right slap and bouf makes an enormous difference to a film. It must do, because bad hair and make-up can totally ruin one.

To wit, the movie version of *I Capture the Castle* (one of my top five all-time favourite books) was destroyed for me by the stupid wig that the actress playing Rose was forced to wear. Likewise Hermione's ridiculous thatch in the early Harry Potter films. The B-52s' classic track 'Wigs on Fire' is all I could think about when I watched those movies. (It goes like this: 'What's that on your head? A wig. Wig! Wig! Wig!' It's legendary.)

The thing is, if a wig makes a person's head look as large as a kewpie doll's and if it has a tell-tale, hide-the-join fringe, you can forget the subtleties and nuances of acting. All you can think is: Wig! Wig! Wig!

Then, just last night, *Cold Mountain* was completely wrecked for me by Nicole Kidman's fingernails. Which was quite an achievement, considering that I am now so in love with Jude Law I might have to desert my family and devote the rest of my life to stalking him.

The irony is that *his* hair and slap totally make the film. You thought he was a cutie as the clean-cut rich kid in *The Talented Mr Ripley*? Well, in my (possibly hormonal) opinion that was nothing on him down and dirty, scarred and bloody as a wounded Confederate soldier. Hoo-wee, pass my fan, Scarlett. You could *smell* the dirt and sweat on him, and I'm first in the queue to . . . Oh, never mind.

Anyway, so there's Jude looking thrillingly filthy, those sensitive pale blue eyes madly emoting out of his unshaven face (oh GOD), and along comes Nicole with a perfect manicure and totally ruins the climax of the entire film. I won't destroy the plot for you, in case you haven't seen it, but it's fairly common knowledge that the story involves Ms Kidman – or Ada Monroe, as she is called in it – living off the land for several years, to survive the American Civil War in a remote mountain settlement.

So she's a-diggin' vegies, a-milkin' cows, a-choppin' wood, a-killin' hogs etc with her bare hands. Yet she has perfect nails – with top coat. Not much to eat up there in Cold Mountain during the killin' an' the fightin' an' all, but clearly an excellent supply of Jessica nail products.

She already had me offside in the opening scenes for wearing copious amounts of eye shadow, eyebrow pencil and mascara, which I really don't think they went in for back in 1861. Especially if you were the refined daughter of a preacherman. But it was the nails that really did me in. (Possibly, also, because they were touching Jude Law.)

Funnily enough, her wigs weren't too distracting and I liked the way that, even at the beginning, before the war, her hair was a bit flyaway and imperfect, so you got the idea that she – Ada, not Nicole – had done it herself.

So what I don't understand is: how could they get that right and the make-up so disastrously wrong? Especially as no other woman in the film seemed to be wearing it.

The wonderful, wacky Renée Zellweger looked like she had been sleeping with the hogs throughout the film and I sincerely hoped she would run off with the Oscar for Best Supporting Actress.*

Or at least, Best Supporting Make-up.

*She did.

Hair way to hell

My partner P. suggested the subject of this column: The Three Stages of Haircuts. His descriptions of them made me laugh so much I decided to have a go at it, although hair traumas are really his special subject. He has suffered very badly with his hair since he was a teenager. It is jet-black, dead straight and thick and likes nothing more than to stand up on end like an Olympic gymnast.

Growing up in communist Yugoslavia in the 1970s, they didn't have much in the way of hair gel (and the film *Something About Mary* hadn't come out yet), so from the age of thirteen onwards, when girls and therefore hair suddenly became hugely important, he developed his own method of taming it.

After washing his hair, he used to pull one of his mother's stockings, with a knot tied in it, over his head while it dried, to make the disobedient hair lie flat against his head. Then he had to hide around the house for several hours in dread fear that a schoolfriend might see him.

I would give almost anything to be transported back in time to see this vision, but the nearest I can get is a photograph of him, aged about sixteen, with shiny black hair clinging to his scalp like cling film, the parting a rather erratic crazy paving path across his head. This, he admits, was a problem with the stocking method.

The irony of this is that at the very time he was creeping about like a drag queen yet to apply her wig, I was trying every manner of gloop to make my soft, fine hair stand up on end in the style demanded by punk rock fashion. If only he had been living in Birmingham, rather than Belgrade, his hair would have been his pride and joy. In fact, I had a boyfriend when I was eighteen who I liked simply because his hair stood up in such a brilliant spiky thatch.

I tried everything from the newly emerging species of 'high hair' products to strong solutions of sugar in water to achieve a similar effect, but the only thing that made my hair stand up even a little bit was several days of dirt and about three cans of extra-strong hairspray. My apologies to the ozone layer.

I have to admit that later in life I have come to give thanks for hair that lies down and behaves itself with fairly minimal effort, but P. still suffers terribly with his. Any important outing requires careful planning for the timing of the hair wash. Once achieved, the wet hair requires special vigorous drying with a hard towel, then combing and parting preparation followed by a special hairdo nap, when he will lie first on one side, then the other, to make it submit to flatness.

Finally comes the application of the gel and artful combing, after which he has the most lovely straight, floppy hair and you would never know about the crisis of mohican crest which has been averted. After these preparations, I am not allowed to touch his hair in any circs.

He suffers also with haircuts, as he has to train hairdressers intensively to understand the wilful nature of his barnet, so from this life-long study of hair trauma, his theory on haircuts is as follows:

Stage One. You've had the haircut and you hate it.

Stage Two. It settles down and looks great. This is a very short period.

Stage Three. You start to look like a wild and woolly Visigoth, until the day when you book another haircut, when it looks perfect in the few hours preceding the appointment.

The sequence then begins again.

The irony of all these follicular agonies is that apart from a very nice black cashmere poloneck, the thing that first attracted me to P. across a crowded party was his beautiful, glossy straight hair.

The Twenty-eight
Ages of Man

During a recent bout of foul chest infection lurgy, I was checking the small print on my medication when I was struck by the instructions relating to various ages. These were divided into 'children under five', 'children under twelve' and then 'adults and the elderly'.

It was the last one that made me stop and think. Why would 'adults' and 'the elderly' be different? Surely 'the elderly' are also adults? I couldn't see why they would make that distinction, unless there were different implications for a) adults and b) the elderly in taking the pills.

It made me vaguely offended on behalf of the so-called elderly, because it sounds as though we pass through adulthood and then come out the other side as elderly, which has a less-than sort of a ring to it. As if on achieving elderlyhood you might have to give back your right to vote and order drinks in a bar.

An image of the grandad from *The Simpsons* flashed into my brain. I could see him going into Moe's Tavern and trying to order a beer and Moe asking him for ID.

'Are you sure you're under ninety-one?'

Then I started wondering when exactly just being an older adult stops and being 'the elderly' starts? Middle age seems to start later and later, so 'the elderly' might not kick in until you are nearly a hundred these days.

Is my mum, now well into her eighties, 'the elderly'? I'm sure it's not a title she would welcome. In fact, I know she would rage against it. It sounds so very frail – both in limb and mind – and while Peggy Senior might be a bit elderly in the hip joints these days, her brain is most definitely still Adult. She's more clued up on current affairs than me most of the time, and a big fan of *Celebrity Big Brother*.

So all these ponderings on the subject of age and the labels we put on ourselves got me to thinking that it might be time for us to redefine the Seven Ages of Man.

These used to be: Infancy, Childhood, Youth, Adulthood, Middle Age, Old, Deathbed. I know this from the model of the Karmic Circle of Life in the window of the Hare Krishna restaurant just off Soho Square in London, which has long been on my list of the Great Free Sights of London Town.

I think it's time the Hare Krishnas did a new model (they have a sort of doll for each age, going round in a circle – it's so interesting), along the following lines – and once I started, seven ages no longer seemed nearly enough. Looking at the childcare books, at not even four years old, my daughter already seems to have passed through four distinct stages.

So here are my proposals for the new Twenty-eight Ages of Man (and Woman):

1. Milk-fed Infant
2. Weaned Infant
3. Toddler
4. Pre-schooler
5. Properly Innocent Early Childhood
6. Knowing Middle Childhood
7. Pre-teen
8. Early Teen
9. Toxic Teen
10. Mature Teen
11. Youth
12. Glorious Gilded Youth
13. Youth in Excelsis
14. Extended Youth
15. Continued Extended Youth
16. Late Continued Extended Youth
17. Mature Youth
18. Early Middle Youth
19. Middle Youth
20. Later Middle Youth
21. Approaching Middle Age
22. Very Early Middle Age
23. Mid-middle Age
24. Mature Middle Age
25. Pre-maturity

26. Maturity
27. Still Marvellous for Your Age
28. The Elderly

I think that just about covers it. The London Hare Krishnas will just have to get a bigger window.

Quilt of many colours

I seem to be assembling a rag bag. So far, I have only used torn-off pieces of the old shirts and pyjamas in it for grubby jobs like cleaning paintbrushes, but some of the things in there really are much too nice for that, which made me remember the other thing people used to do with their rag bags – make patchwork quilts.

I've got a lovely one myself which I found in a junk shop years ago. It's not one of those beautiful American ones in a fiendishly clever tessellated pattern; in fact it's more like crazy paving than tiling.

But I love it even more for its rough-hewn quality; it's much more personal than one of those perfect ones. With its quirky mix of fabrics and quite clumsy stitches, that quilt is almost like a book of short stories to me.

I've got it over a sofa in the bathroom and I lie in the bath staring at it and wondering what tales it has to tell. There are so many disparate kinds of fabric there.

There are quite a few pieces from what were clearly

a man's stripy business shirts. Was it one man or two? A husband or a son? A father, even. Then I wonder what kind of job he did to wear those shirts. Or were they just for Sunday best? Either way, I can see them going through a mangle, hanging on a line, and being pressed with a flat iron off the stove.

Then there are pretty printed florals, which must have been summer dresses, and from the 1930s, judging by the style of the prints. I can see those dresses going on picnics and on charabancs to the seaside, walking along the seafront, eating an ice-cream on the pier.

There are some fabric pieces with the same print in different colourways. So did she get some remnants from a fabric shop? I'm sure the dresses were homemade. I can see her in that shop, looking at the pattern books and feeling the 'stuff', as they used to call it in those days.

There are other prints which look as though they come from children's clothes. Little summer dresses and romper suits. How hard it must have been to cut them up to make the quilt pieces – or maybe she waited until they had been passed down and washed and worn so many times that it was all they were good for.

Which makes me wonder how long it took her to assemble all the fabric for that quilt. It's big enough to cover a double bed, with different patches on each side, none the same touching, which adds up to quite a metre-age.

So was it made by an older woman from her rag bag when all her family had left home? A memento of her busy years, which helped to pass the time when the nest was suddenly empty (I'm starting to well up a bit, in the bath, by this point).

Or did a mother give the rag bag to her daughter to make a quilt for her bottom drawer, ready to go on the marital bed, primed with memories of her childhood? (More welling.)

Mind you, in the pre-telly era – and we can't be talking any later than the early 1950s here – people did have more time on their hands of an evening. Even a mother of young children might have liked a project to pass the time. Or maybe it was made in the war years. It certainly has that sense of thrift about it. Anything to take your mind off the waiting and the worrying.

I'll never know, of course, but I love to wonder. And it makes me think that instead of heaving everything into the charity bin, perhaps we should all make such a quilt. I like the idea of snuggling beneath my memories.

Rock and rule

The other day I was at the luggage carousel waiting for my bag to come off a flight from Melbourne when I realised I was standing next to the Rolling Stones circa 1968. Or Led Zeppelin in 1974. Or Guns and Roses circa 1988. Or The Verve circa 1997. Or Razorlight circa 2006.

Whoever they actually were, even before the guitar cases starting chugging round the conveyor belt, it was blatantly apparent they were a rock band, because of the hilarious clothes they were wearing. Not to mention the surly over-it-don't-look-at-me attitude. But why would you dress like that if being looked at wasn't what you really craved?

Anyway, I was blatantly looking at them. I was loving them. They were my kind of boys. They all had don't-give-a-shit hair – which probably took some time to achieve – most of them were wearing silly sunglasses (indoors, remember) and one sported a denim butcher boy cap (Bob Dylan 1962) with the insouciance that can only be assumed when you wear a daft hat every single day. Another had on a T-shirt clearly picked up off a girlfriend's bedroom floor. It was so too small for him there was a wide expanse of white, hairy belly between the bottom of it and the start of his too-tight faded hipster jeans.

It was all classic rock gear and I so adored those young men for wearing it. They would have had no idea how happy they had made an old lady, because they reminded me how much I love rock style.

I do really actually love it, but it also amuses me intensely. What I enjoy is the way every new wave of bands assumes this identikit rock 'n' roll style and then acts as though they have invented it, when in fact it has been going strong for over forty years.

The attitude those chaps at the airport were copping, you'd think they were making some kind of big, dangerous, rebellious statement – look ma, no shoe polish! – when really it's just a uniform. It's as conventional in its way as a London gent in his pinstripe suit and bowler hat, or an Aussie bloke in his Blundies and King Gee shorts.

In the same way, that guy Scott Weiland from Velvet Revolver had me absolutely hysterical with his posturing at Live 8, like he was the first skinny rocker ever to wear a cat-suit and a stupid hat. David Bowie was doing all that – and much more – thirty-five years ago, yet Mr Weiland seemed almost in awe of his own brilliantly naughty fabulousness. There was a naivety to it that I found rather endearing (whilst also wanting to push him, fully clothed, into the nearest swimming pool).

It reminded me of my nephew Chris's mid-teen obsession with Marilyn Manson. He once forced me to watch a long documentary about Mr M, so I could appreciate how totally amazing he is, but while I do admire his intelligence (he made a brilliant contribution to Michael Moore's film *Bowling for Columbine*, if you saw that), I couldn't find much truly original about his onstage style. But my nephew thought he was the second coming.

I whispered my disappointment to his dad, my brother Nick. 'That Marilyn Manson – there's nothing new about him,' I said. 'It's new to him,' said Nick, which I thought was terribly wise.

When I was a young rocker in the late seventies I can remember looking at pictures of Lou Reed and his gang taken ten years earlier and actively emulating their look of stripy T-shirts, leather jackets and skinny pants. And they were already channelling Marlon Brando in *The Wild One* from over ten years before that. Really, there is nothing new in the rock style canon. What's new is the people adopting it each time.

So just as each generation thinks that they have invented sex, each generation thinks they have invented rock rebellion, and therein lies the unbridled joy of it.

Closet queen

As a child I had a fantasy about being accidentally locked into Harrods one night and being able to play freely in all the departments – particularly toys, ladies' shoes, children's clothes and pets – before heading down to the food hall's chocolate room to sustain myself. I would be found the next morning, I imagined, in an organdie-draped four-poster princess bed in the furniture department, several empty chocolate boxes beside me. A lion cub would be sleeping at my feet.

In adult life this daydream has developed into a strong desire to perve at the wardrobes of the world's chicest women. I long to see inside Kate Moss's closets, for example. Apart from fingering the actual clothes and accessories, I would love to see how she stores all her gear. I can't help thinking that it just might all be thrown in there (and I have seen inside one of her hotel rooms, when I was doing an interview with her many years ago, so I know of what I speak).

Anna Wintour, on the other hand, whose closets I also

long to throw open, I can imagine taking more of an archival approach. Is it all folded with acid-free tissue in special museum-quality boxes? Or hanging inside special moth-proof canvas garment bags? Are there separate cedar-lined closets for summer and winter clothes? What are the hangers like? How does she store her handbags?

I would also love to know how such a fashion icon keeps tricky things like scarves and gloves, so that they stay nice, but you can also see what you have. It's very easy to forget a favourite silk square if it's hidden under a carefully folded pile of others, which you don't want to mess up scratching through them like a busy dog, as you'd only have to fold them again, which would make you late for work (or I would, anyway).

Other wardrobes I long to get accidentally locked into belong to Loulou de la Falaise, Madonna, Amanda Harlech, Naomi Campbell, Victoria Beckham, Liz Hurley, Lil' Kim and Cher.

On the male side, I'd like to see if Manolo Blahnik's closets are as much like Jay Gatsby's as I imagine. I do so picture neat stacks of perfectly laundered shirts and ranks of immaculate shoes. I have similar visions of P Diddy's arrangements. But how does Mick Jagger store his gear? Bryan Ferry? Keef?

But while harbouring these little flights of fancy I actually know that the reality of raking through someone else's clothing does not live up to the dream. In fact, there is something strangely depressing about other people's wardrobes.

I have had the chance over the years to inspect the contents of some of very chic closets for professional reasons – usually because I was writing an article about their Fabulous Home – and far from revealing the mysteries of the well-dressed, checking out another person's wardrobe can make you wonder how they ever get out of the house at all.

Because even the most expensive and beautiful clothes look terribly sad and lifeless just hanging there. Without the colour or styling themes of a boutique, there is always the defeated air of the 'nearly new' store about it. Or of a wardrobe that must be cleared after a death. A musty smell hangs around any clothes that have ever been worn, even in the most immaculate households. It's so disappointing.

But while it is disheartening to acknowledge that even a rake through Madonna's threads could be a downer, there are two notions that spring from this realisation that I find quite inspiring. Firstly, that any item of clothing, once worn, somehow takes on an indelible emotional trace of the person who has worn it. If you have ever found an old but unworn item in a vintage shop, you will know it doesn't have the same poignant air as pre-loved attire. It's quite strange. And the second understanding is that, in fact, clothes do not make the man – or woman – but that it takes a human personality to bring a garment to life.

In a time where we are increasingly led to believe that elegance, along with all other aspects of fulfilment, can be bought off the peg, I find that rather comforting.

Me Vintage

I've written before about something I call Me Vintage.

At least, I think I've written about it before. I know I meant to, but just this morning I couldn't remember the name of the Duke of Windsor ('You know, the one who had to stop being king, because he wanted to marry the divorced woman; no, not Prince Charles, the other one . . .'), so maybe I just meant to and never actually did. Really, my brain's got more holes in it than a Bottega Veneta woven leather tote these days, so I can't be sure of anything.

Anyway, Me Vintage is when fashion does one of its little backflips and something you already have in the back of your wardrobe suddenly becomes totally right again and you can just pull it out and pop it on and everyone says, 'Aren't you marvellous?' And you say, 'This? It's vintage.'

Then you can just leave that notion hanging there, happy in the knowledge that they are probably picturing you in Didier Ludot in Paris, or Relik in London, rummaging through the rails next to Kate Moss. When actually you got your dark navy nautical jacket with gold braid trim – à la this-season Balenciaga – out of a black bin liner on top of your wardrobe. It's positively fiendish.

The other version of it is when someone says, 'What tremendous bangles. I've been looking everywhere for some just like that. Where did you get them?' and you smile quietly and say, 'Oh, I've had these for twenty years . . .'

Then you get a faraway look in your eye and continue: 'I bought these four from a peddler on a beach in Mauritius; that one was a present from a Fendi sister – can't remember which one – and I got the other one in Top Shop, back in the day. Or was it New York . . .?'

I love that. It makes me feel like Karen Blixen, or Peggy Guggenheim. Old and weathered, but in a good way. It's just about the only time I'm happy about being on the wrong side of forty.

The Swan Moment

I have written before about the terrible misfortune of being fourteen, but now I have a happier tale to tell. I have recently observed at very close hand a wonderful thing that happens to people shortly after they are fourteen – let's call it the Swan Moment.

A dear friend of mine is fifteen, very nearly sixteen, and I swear her Swan Moment happened overnight. I watched it like one of those pieces of time-lapse photography where they show you a rose unfurling. Except this was a Lily, which is the name of my friend.

When I first met her she was fourteen and she was, well, she was pretty gawky. Although she had a lovely face and enviably long limbs, the face had spots on it and the limbs were sort of put on wrong. You know how Michael Caine's arms can look a bit back to front? That's how Lily's long legs were.

Then one evening I opened the door and this beautiful young woman was standing there. She didn't have spots and she had wonderful slinky legs in a groovy denim mini, her hair was sleek and soigné, and I swear I did a real double-take, like someone in a cartoon. It was Lily. I didn't say anything at first, as I didn't want to embarrass her, but in the end I just had to blurt it out.

'Lily,' I said. 'You've changed.'

'I know,' she said.

'You've got all beautiful,' I said.

She shrugged. 'It just sort of happened over the last few months and suddenly everyone's noticed. My spots have gone.'

But it was much more than that. It was like the spots moved out and the glamour fairy moved in. Just like that. Ever since, I have thought of that evening as The Night They Invented Champagne, as the whole thing was pure *Gigi*, although not so pervy (that film has always totally given me the creeps).

I still see Lily most days, as she lives on my street and she helps me out with stuff like filing, but really because I just like having her around, and the amazing thing is that the Swan Moment just keeps on going.

Every time I open the door she looks more lovely. There's a gloss going on now, an added enhancement that is more than just an absence of spots. It's like living in a fairytale, watching it all.

When I think about it, I have observed later stages of the Swan Moment before, when young girls have come to work with me on fashion magazines. They arrive already fashion-aware, or I wouldn't have given them the job, but still a little gauche, a touch raw and provincial.

It always used to delight me to watch the magic of being surrounded by some seriously sophisticated and stylish people do its work on a new recruit. A new haircut, done by a world-famous cutter on a fashion shoot, was often the start, then a different make-up look, a few designer clothes passed on by a kind fashion editor and then, after some exposure to press discount and sample sales, you would see the duckling move into full fashionista mode and off she'd fly. A superb swan.

And in retrospect I can remember it happening to me too, although I don't remember a teenage Swan Moment, like Lily's, as I was always too obsessed with how ugly I was.

What I can clearly recall, though, is lightbulb moments of understanding about how to dress and shop like a grown-up, from when I first started working on magazines. In fact, I think I am still learning all that; it's a never-ending process, but I am all too aware that I no longer have the rest of the package to fully showcase the new revelations.

The juncture of youth and sophistication that is the Swan Moment is truly a glorious thing. And as fleeting as a summer.

The God of Small Things

Sometimes all it takes is one tiny scrap of chiffon to change your life. Well, maybe not quite your life, but it can certainly make you feel a whole lot jauntier as you go around your usual drudge.

The particular piece of fabric I am referring to here is in the form of a funny old scarf I found the other weekend in an op shop. It's a really beautiful bit of vintage chiffon, which somebody clever has fashioned into a long, narrow scarf. It's certainly a home-sewing machine job, but it's been deftly done, so that it is cut on the bias, with three separate pieces joined so that the bias is going in different directions where they meet, with the ends sliced on the diagonal.

Little details like that can have an almost Pinocchio effect on a piece of fabric – the turning into a boy bit, not the nose – giving it a kind of vitality of its own, as the fabric pulls and dances in different directions. A small and magical fact of physics that John Galliano has a firm grasp on.

On top of that clever cutting, it's the most amazing graphic

Futurist jazz print, in an absolutely perfect flame-red and French navy, with just-off white. It really is nothing more than a scrap, yet it has boosted my whole wardrobe into this season. And done equivalent wonders for my mood.

Nautical – with a particular reference to 'Riviera Style' – is a key trend right now and this scarf sums it up. Fling it on with my favourite white jeans (which you can wear year-round now; the not-after-Easter rule is so totally over), a navy pique pea coat, a long-sleeved navy T-shirt and my oldest Prada bag (nearly twenty years and still going strong, can you believe it?) with its bang-on-trend chain straps and I feel totally there.

And I think it is because this tiny little scarf is so narrow and the fabric so outrageously lightweight that I feel I am doing it in a subtle way. I'm referencing Riviera Style, rather than dressing up in it for an am dram production of *Private Lives*.

Another feature of this wonder accessory is that it has an extraordinary ability just to keep that little bit of edge in the wind off your neck, so you feel exactly warm enough, without getting overheated. And I also can't help hoping that the draw-the-eye-downwards dangly nature of it might make me look that little bit elongated too. I feel taller in it, anyway. The fact that it cost the princely sum of $5 has done nothing to mar its charm, either.

The only thing that is enervating me about amazer-scarf is obsessing on what kind of garment it came from – and what happened to the rest of it. I reckon it was either some kind of fabulous afternoon dress, or a blouse to be worn with wide pants and a cheeky little hat. Definitely wedges on the feet. It's the sort of scrap that could inspire an entire collection for a properly creative designer, and right now it is fully inspiring me.

This is not the only time that one little accessory has boosted my entire wardrobe. Last season (or was it the one before? They meld in my brain) I bought a necklace of large pebble-like black beads on a piece of narrow ribbon for a very modest sum in a chain store. It was an impulse buy, but every time I put it on, I felt my outfit had been snapped right into the Lanvin zone, where I would very much like to dwell.

So bear this in mind, as you are flicking through the glossy mags, so full of 'key pieces' you 'need' for the new season. While it might be lovely to acquire a whole new wardrobe every autumn and spring, sometimes all you really need is one tiny thing. Less really can be more.

True colours

I can sing a rainbow, but I don't speak Mouse. I'm talking here, specifically, about paint colour, and in that regard people seem to divide into Rainbow or Mouse speakers.

When I'm choosing how to decorate a room it pretty much comes down to this (and roughly in this order of preference): yellow, pink, blue, cream, green, or dark red. That's it; those are room colours, as far as I'm concerned.

And when I do a mental inventory of my house I have rooms in all of them, with the exception of dark red – although I've got designs on the dining room in that regard.

People visiting for the first time often comment, while putting on their sunglasses, that I'm 'not afraid of colour', and it's true. My hallways are art deco green, my daughter's playroom is 'Kinky Pink' (that really is the official name of the shade) and the paint on my sitting room walls is called 'Sunflower Explosion'. It's a mighty, mighty yellow.

Mostly, it delights me, all this colour (and did I mention that I have some chairs in that yellow sitting room in a not-at-all bashful pink devoré velvet?). But then I go to the houses of some of my more tasteful friends and I feel distinctly less-than.

These are people so fluent in Mouse, they can spot the difference between shades of Mole, Seal and Donkey at 100 metres. When they're choosing paint they have a whole extra spectrum to choose from, of colours so subtle they don't even register on my vulgar retinas.

I'm not talking here about bland cop-out choices, like the dreaded Magnolia, but truly sophisticated shades. If you were to define Mouse colours, they are all the ones where you're not quite sure if it's brown or grey, or green or blue.

So you couldn't just say, 'It's in the yellow room', or 'the pink room', as I do, you'd have to say, 'It's in the room that's a marvellous sort of Oat, mixed with Pebble and a touch of Hazelnut.' But Mouse speakers just take one look and say: 'Oh, Shiitake.'

And it's not just the walls that get the benefit of these sophisticated mixes. Mousers are so clever at using teaming and toning shades of String and Putty and Cricket Pad on woodwork, whereas in my technicolour world, there are only two colours for doors, skirting boards etc: the colour of the walls, or white.

Now, I can do shades of white and cream. I do get that. Some off-whites are dingy, whereas others seem to bounce light around the place, and the only way to find out which is which is to paint large pieces of card with the various possibilities and then hold them up on each wall of the room at different times of day.

But while I can appreciate those subtleties, I just can't do it with the full gamut of Mouse colours – even though I love them, they all swim before my eyes and choosing is impossible. The differences are just too subtle. It's really annoying.

When I go to my friend Hilary's house I could purr at the relaxed elegance of her colour combos. They're so calming to be amongst, whereas my sitting room is a bit like being inside a bag of boiled lollies.

It's odd really, because I can speak Mouse fluently when it comes to clothes. In fact, I'm much happier with Camel and Taupe and Chocolate for my wardrobe than I would be with the circus colours I paint on my walls. It makes no sense.

So I've had an idea. I'm not going to paint the dining room dark red. I'm going to hold my favourite jumpers up against it and then find a paint that matches the one I like best. It will be a paint colour version of a phrase book.

Chop wood, carry water

Do you ever feel you just can't match up one more pair of socks? Can't fold up one more T-shirt, or hang up one more pair of trousers by their ankles? Or put in one more pair of bloody shoe trees?

I do. Right now I think I will spontaneously combust if ever again I have to hang up the towels tidily and put my bath-robe back on its hook and the shampoo back on the shelf. But I know I'll have to. I'll have to do it again tomorrow morning. Because that's what life is made of. Those endlessly repeated little routines.

It never stops. Before I go to bed tonight I'll have to cleanse, tone and moisturise. I'll have to clean and floss my teeth, rub in hand cream, paying special attention to the cuticles, and put cocoa butter on my cracked heels. On a good night, I'll even put on eye cream using gentle taps of the ring finger in the delicate eye area. Then I'll collapse into bed and dream of tidying the towels all over again in the morning.

I have measured out my life in coffee spoons, said J Alfred Prufrock, or rather T S Eliot, his creator. That line has always really struck a chord with me. Even though I drink tea. But it's the same thing. Fill kettle. Kettle on. Mug out. Tea bag in. Water in. Milk in. Tea bag out. Do the hokey-pokey and turn about. Smash the kitchen up with a sledgehammer and run screaming naked through David Jones cosmetics hall.

Aaaah, I feel better now.

I'm not even a commuter with a boring job, who has to get the same train every morning in the same suit, but I still feel this way and I know I'm not alone here on Planet Tedium.

A friend of mine at university said he wanted to invent a machine that would trim his hair, cut his toenails and floss his teeth in a set-up similar to Woody Allen's orgasmatron. You'd just step in, push the button, the machine would do the work and out you'd pop, groomed.

Then just the other day I got a most inspiring letter from a friend who is somewhere he never meant to be – prison. Far from raging against his fate, he is looking resolutely on the positive side and said he finds it quite blissful not to have to think about watering the plants and putting his shoe trees in, which gave me the whole idea for this column.

I thought this condition of routine rage might be what they call 'ennui', but I looked that up in the dictionary and it means listlessness caused by a lack of occupation, not an overload of repetition. (It would be a good name for a perfume, actually, wouldn't it? Ennui, by Gucci. For the really spoilt woman with a large household staff.)

Of course I could just stop doing it all, but what would ensue is chaos and I know that would make me feel even worse. And while I sit here fuming about the clean clothes sorting I know awaits me downstairs (I did it *yesterday*!), I also know at heart that it is these repeated action patterns that really make up the meaningful fabric of our existences, not the holidays of a lifetime, the dream weddings, the big bash birthday parties and the bungee jumps.

Chop wood, carry water, said the Buddha. Meaning that the path to enlightenment comes through repeating the mundane but essential routines of life, rather than in some great flash of insight. A piece of wisdom which I'm happy to admit I got from Van Morrison, rather than the Dalai Lama.

Which reminds me. I have to go and re-file the CDs after the baby pulled them all out of their alphabeticised shelves this afternoon. But first, I think I'll have another cup of tea . . .

Pearly queen

I've got new teeth. They're Swedish. And it was worth waiting two terrible weeks with a gobful of temporary crowns,
which made me feel like Dick Emery dressed up as his vicar
character, for them to arrive by special courier from across
the planet, because my new teeth show all the characteristics of discreet modern design associated with that great
Scandinavian nation. They're sleek and pale, with no rough
edges, like something straight out of John Pawson's house.

Really, I've never seen anything so glamorous as my new
choppers. Not so long ago I could have been a mouth double
for Austin Powers, with my terrible dentistry. Now I look
like Tom Cruise (in the dark). I can't wait to get them on a
dance floor under an ultraviolet light. I'll glow like Casper
the Friendly Ghost.

But quite apart from the look of them – pearly, regular, expensive – it's the feel of them that is so marvellous.
They're as smooth as polished marble and sit flush against
my gums, as perfectly fitted as corn kernels on a cob. The

terrific thing about that is it means there are no longer any sharp edges for passing pieces of food to snag on. With my previous teeth I had reached the stage where I couldn't relax at the dinner table, for fear that I had a floret of broccoli, or a chicken leg, caught on my incisor like a dolphin in a shark net. Half the time I would have my hand over my mouth for fear of giving offence, and that really slows up your witty repartee, I can tell you.

Before my new crowns, the spaces between my teeth were so jagged, even flossing to remove such dinnertime detritus was a nightmare. There were times when I felt like calling emergency services to rescue the dental tape trapped between them.

So why did I suffer so long with teeth I could hardly take out in public? Simple – the terrifying cost of fixing them up. Two crowns and four porcelain veneers cost the same as a small car – or eight pairs of Prada shoes and two bags, as I tend to look at it.

And somehow, while I'm willing to go into debt for high heels (foolish, foolish woman), I had this obsession that I had to Save Up for my teeth. So, of course, that took several years, because I kept spending the tooth fairy's money by accident on trips to Milan's luxury shopping Bermuda Triangle.

Mind you, in terms of instant reaction, I was right about the designer accessories being better value. I have had people cross crowded parties to inspect a new handbag, but no-one has commented on my teeth yet, unless I've approached them grinning like a werewolf, pointing at my mouth and crying, 'Ook! Oo heeth!'

But while I am slightly disappointed they aren't having the 'But, but, you're bewdaful!' effect on people, as seen in old movies when the leading man removes the frumpy secretary's spectacles, deep down I know this is the ultimate compliment to my new gnashers. Because – like facelifts and nose jobs – great teeth are the ones you don't notice.

If someone came up to me now and said, 'Wow, what amazingly perfect white teeth you have', I'd know they were dodgy. It would mean I had one of those brighter than white denture smiles, or those obviously repaired teeth you often see that look like bunches of bananas or sticks of chalk.

Okay, my new teeth were witheringly expensive. But what price can you put on confidence? So if you are walking around with a cakehole full of old piano keys, as I was, stump up and get your teeth done. It really is worth it. Especially as, unlike even your best Prada shoes, you wear them every day.

Interiors monologue

There are few things I enjoy more in life than a good interiors magazine. I love fashion magazines as well, of course, but being a long-time professional Fash Mag Slag, I'm always on alert when I read them, so there is an element of homework about the experience.

But 'shelter magazines', as Americans weirdly call them, are pure, unalloyed pleasure. Unless I make the mistake of allowing my eye to stray from the pictures to the copy. A lot of tripe is written in the name of fashion (and I should know), but I really think that home mags take the Oscar for Best Original Claptrap.

You'll find all kinds of nonsense about 'the new mood in flooring', but the bits that get me really raged up are the articles about 'real' people and their fabulous living environments – and that's just the kind of stupid word they use: not house, or unit, but 'environment', and 'vessel' instead of vase.

The funny thing is that while these real homes are the

kind of pictures I most enjoy looking at in homes magazines, when you read the commentary that goes with them
the people always sound so unbearably smug and thrilled
with themselves and the very cleverness of their witty,
vessel-filled environments. I want to club them to death.
(And then move into their houses and wee in their vessels.)

And it's not just the content; interiors mags have a prose
style that is all their own. People never buy things, they
'source' them, 'discover' them, or 'unearth' them. As in:
'Wilhelmina discovered her ancient Slovakian doorknobs in
a scrapyard in Budapest.' 'Lionel sourced his untanned goat
hair rug on a dung heap in Rajasthan.' 'Priscilla unearthed
her vessels at an agricultural fair in Tamworth.'

They're just fancy names for shopping. Even worse are
their stupid dumb collections, or rather 'passions': 'Lionel
is passionate about cheese graters.' 'Priscilla has an exten-
sive collection of vessels.' 'Wilhelmina combs clinical waste
bins to find new treasures for her large collection of false
teeth – a passion since childhood.'

These are made up, of course, but check out this real
example: 'After selecting some exotic glasses, plates and sil-
verware from her vast collection, [Laura] decorates the table
with vegetables, herbs or fruits from the garden, adding
things she has collected during walks in the forest: almond
husks, leaves, seeds, rocks, or flowers. Sometimes she will
pour powdered spices onto the table.' Oh, pass my club. And
what about this one: ' "I collect oil paintings of people in red
clothing," says Ellen.' But why?

Mind you, it's not really fair that these people should bear the full weight of my scorn, as it's not entirely their fault that they come over sounding like such total arses. I know this from experience. My house was once photographed for a magazine.

Of course, my ego was swollen beyond belief at the idea of actually appearing in one of the mags I love so much, and I was delighted to let them into my environment (and promote one of my books in the process). But I made one great mistake.

After I had done the necessary posing by my mantelpiece (covered with artefacts sourced, unearthed and found, including several witty vessels – a passion), I left them to it. 'Do whatever you want,' I said, as I breezed out. Biiiiiig blunder.

When the article was published, I was thrilled how super they made my house look. Much nicer than it actually was. But then I saw that in one shot my bedside table was empty except for a shallow vessel of water with flower heads floating in it. I cringed a million cringes. It made me look like such a pretentious git.

My bedside table is always piled high with books, magazines, bits torn out of newspapers and scribble pads. Why wouldn't it be? I'm a writer. That picture made me look like an empty vessel, more interested in the look of things than the sense of them.

Hmmmm, maybe they were on to something.

Do it yourself

I recently saw a gripping British reality (whatever that is) TV program about a normal (whatever that is) family of four, who agreed to live without using a supermarket for a fortnight, just to see what would happen. Oh, how they suffered!

Mummy Bear's full-time job was actually on the checkout of a major supermarket chain, where she also did all the family grocery shopping – and I mean *all*. The household diet consisted entirely of frozen ready meals, with side orders of frozen chips and frozen peas, with frozen apple pie and ice-cream for pudding, all served piping hot (apart from the ice-cream) direct from mama's microwave. The closest they ever got to fresh food was McDonald's, and all these delicious repasts were taken on the collective knee in front of the television.

By the middle of the first week Mummy Bear was ready to go into a nursing home, she was so exhausted and frustrated. It had taken her all day to source the ingredients for her first from-scratch meal since school domestic science lessons, and the resulting Lancashire hotpot did not make it onto the kitchen table until 10.30 pm.

The expression on the Baby Bears' faces when they saw it was priceless. A steaming plate of stewed sandshoes could not have provoked greater revulsion. It was hilarious. How I gloated!

I could sit and scoff at them, in middle-class *Vogue Entertaining* self-satisfaction, because apart from Sirena tuna, I rarely buy actual food in supermarkets, considering such establishments useful only as purveyors of washing powder, bin liners, roach motels, pan scourers and light bulbs.

In my world, you buy bread, cheese, tea bags, ham, olive oil and biscuits from overpriced but deeply committed delis, meat from one particular Italian butcher, and everything else from Macro Wholefoods. Which means I probably spend about 46 per cent of our household income on food (as the French do, apparently), whereas the average Brit family, like the one I was watching, spends something like 11 per cent. Most of it on artificial colouring, by the looks of it.

But as I sat there, smugly sponging the last bit of designer olive oil from my plate with a crust of $8 bread, it occurred to me just how lost I would be without clothes shops.

It would take a bit longer to reduce me to the flaming-cheeked and prickly-eyed frustration visible on Mummy Bear as she realised she had to go to one shop for the potatoes and another for the chump chops, or to work up to her fury at discovering, shortly before family tea, that bread dough has to prove for quite some time before you can bake it, but my first attempt at cutting out a pair of pants would do it.

I hate sewing. Hate it. It's so slow. I can't bear things you can't do quickly – or do something else at the same time. While bread dough is proving you can do the crossword, or weed a border. If you try to hurry sewing – or watch a Doris Day movie at the same time – you always end up with one sleeve on backward. I can't tell you the number of times I've jumped up and down like Rumpelstiltskin after carefully basting a hem up on the outside of a skirt.

But maybe necessity would force me, over time, to become a handy home dressmaker and a natty knitter. By the end of the supermarket show, the Baby Bears were fighting over Mummy's homemade bread, while she gutted a freshly caught fish.

You may see me crocheting yet.

Toddler chic

The other night I bathed my daughter as usual. Dried her little cracks and crevices. Counted toes. Blew raspberries on neck. Then something terrible happened. She put on her own pyjamas. Just like that, with no kind of a warning, just boom – 'Look Mummy, I dressed myself!'

I confess I hid behind her (sugar-pink) towel and wept. She even got them on the right way round and she was so proud of herself. I was simply gutted. It was such a poignant reminder that one day I just won't be needed.

Now, I do clearly recall what seems like just a few months ago, lamenting how hard it is to dress a young toddler who does not wish to co-operate. Especially when small buttons are involved. I likened the venture to trying to play the piano while holding an angry possum. That stage was very difficult, but it doesn't mean I'm ready for her to start dressing herself.

Especially as she is now – or was until just the other night – at the perfect stage of cuddly dressability. She co-operates so sweetly, snuggling on my lap with pointed feet and extending arms and then in a flash, we were over 'helping mummy to dress me', and on to 'dressing myself'.

I should have seen it coming, really, as her best pal Bella is exactly five months older and a living weathervane of the developmental changes that are just ahead for Peggy. For quite a while now, Bella has been putting on her own pyjamas. Sometimes at three in the afternoon. Because she can.

And I should take note of what she's up to and get prepared – possibly with locks on the wardrobe door. We were over there yesterday for tea and Bella changed her clothes five times. Sometimes she'll tip a perfectly good cup of apple juice down her front just as an excuse to slip into a different look.

The other shift now taking hold with Bella is towards strong opinions about what she wants to wear. The other morning her mum wanted to put her in black tights and she refused violently, stating, 'Mummy, I'm blonde – I can't wear black tights.'

I've already had my first taste of this with young Peggy, when we were in a really nice little girls' clothes shop looking for a special dress for her third birthday party.

I found two I liked – a bold pink-and-white check number with a lovely sticky-out petticoat, and a really beautiful traditional white dress with pink smocking. I couldn't decide which I liked best and, out of whimsy more than anything, I asked Peggy for her opinion.

'I'm not wearing *that*,' she said, with withering contempt, when I held up the one with the smocking. 'That's for babies.'

I bought the checked one, because I really didn't think I'd ever get her into the other one – and that was when I realised how short a time I have left to dictate what she wears. Judging by Bella, it can only be a matter of months before she is simply refusing to wear things she doesn't like.

This could very slightly break my heart. OK, my husband may be right when he says she is my dolly, but I have so adored choosing her little clothes – a whole new wardrobe each season, what a thrill! – and putting them together in little outfits.

Not that I have ever wanted her to be one of those ostentatiously overdressed children. She has never worn Burberry, for instance. Equally, I'm not keen on those mini fashion plates, who are really togged up to accessorise the parent – I hate it when you see kids overstyled with bandannas and the like.

So I'm just going to make the most of controlling her clothes while I can. Although, looking on the bright side, once she starts choosing her own outfits, I'll have a lot more time back to devote to my own.

Spoiled goods

When, exactly, did I turn into Princess Pom Pom? When, for example, and why, did it become essential for me to have just about every item of laundry in my house – even tea towels – crisply ironed and folded? By someone else.

I survived years of adult life barely touching an iron and wouldn't have dreamed of paying somebody to do it for me. I would have thought it a profligate waste of money that could be spent on high heels and cocktails and the other pressing concerns of one's sweet and twenties.

Instead, I deliberately avoided clothes which required such meticulous attention and seemed to find unironed pillowslips and doona covers perfectly acceptable to sleep among. Now, though, the very thought of a bed made up in such an unkempt student manner makes me feel quite nervous.

I can't decide whether age has just made me unbearably bourgeois and suburban in my values ('I have always so admired your whites, Doreen – which washing powder do you use?'); or whether it is a kind of greater discernment that has come with experience.

Certainly spending a fair amount of my working life ensconced in fairly decent hotels and a few five-star resorts has upped my Pom Pom ante. You do get used to a good level of thread count if you stay in nice places. And to having fresh sheets and towels every day. And your undies and socks coming back from the laundry service ironed.

Really, after intense exposure to all that, I can see how someone like J.Lo, once just Jenny from the Block, could have become over time such a Thread Count Tyrant. It's in her rider, allegedly (the list of conditions promoters have to agree to if they want her to show up), that all bed linen in Miss Lopez's vast suite must be at least 300 threads per square inch.

I'm sure her mama didn't teach little Jen Jen about thread counts back when she was still from the block. It's just not something you encounter until you drift up to quite a lofty plane of consumer karma – about the same level where you can spot the difference between real Champagne and mere sparkling wine, just by the speed of the bubbles in the glass. And identify Krug from Moët with your eyes closed. You can't just buy that level of discernment; you can only acquire it with experience.

So I am inclined to think my Pom Pom-ism is adult-onset learned behaviour. Or in simpler terms: it comes with age. I certainly can't claim that my aversion to such déclassé items as man-made fibres is a result of a childhood wrapped in cashmere, Irish linen and pima cotton. Rather, I grew up during the height (depth?) of the space-race era, where anything made from plastics was considered vastly superior, and 'natural' translated as backward and primitive.

I remember homemade dresses of terrifying textiles so dense and unbreathable you could have used them as shower curtains. And for many years I slept between brushed nylon sheets, which were pretty much like flocked cling film. Not pleasant on a hot summer night, but if you didn't know anything else you just got on with it. And I can certainly see why my mother embraced them so enthusiastically. Sheets that came out of the washer almost as dry as they went in must have seemed an unbelievable bonus for a mother of four.

But despite growing up with all that, I can now spot a trace of polyester in a sheet at fifty metres and recoil from it like a vampire from a head of garlic. I have been known to check out of a hotel just because it had poly-cotton bedclothes.

Yet, while I am at times slightly nauseated by my own Princess Pom Pom standards, I like to think of it as a form of connoisseurship. Otherwise I might have to face up to the fact that I'm just plain spoiled.

Size matters

You know those surveys they do every few years which reveal that 90 per cent of women are wearing the wrong size bra? I reckon they could broaden them out and find that 90 per cent of us are wearing the wrong size clothing too.

I have only recently fully understood how crucial an issue choosing sizes is in looking – and feeling – your best. And I'm not just talking about those horrendous moments when you discover you have gone up to the next level of hell with one of your regular brands; there's more to it than that.

While those horrendous 'Oh, so I really *am* fat' changing room epiphanies are just about the only thing that could ever put me off shopping for very long, there are other, less obvious pitfalls.

These might not be such a tangible boot to the self-esteem as discovering you are now barely squeezing into size 14 Country Road pants, but they can quietly chip away at your confidence at an almost subliminal level.

One of the worst is buying clothes that are too big. Trust

me on this. Because I have had several periods in my life when I was approaching full Fat Bastard status, when offered an array of T-shirts from Extra Small to Extra Large, I will reach for the Large every time, because I just assume I am at the tubby end of the scale.

There is, of course, also the issue that I would rather try something on and find it is too big than find it is too small. But while starting with the bigger sizes is OK with a skirt, or pants, because if they're falling off you it's pretty obvious and so you try a smaller size, with T-shirts, knits and dresses it's all a bit amorphous.

As long as you can get it over your head, any size of T-shirt 'fits' and in the 1980s I recall that very oversized ones (with the sleeves rolled up to your armpits and a pair of stretch leggings below) were very much the go. But that was then. Now you want a T-shirt that fits you neatly, but I keep buying them too big.

I did this last week and while I loved my new Splendid top, once I got it home I knew it didn't look quite right. The shoulders were funny, it was way too long and it kind of stuck out at the sides, which wasn't terribly flattering. In fact, it made me look fatter than I am. But it took me a while to realise that this was because it was actually too big for me. A smaller size might have revealed the odd sausage of fat around my middle when I sat down, but it would still have looked better than the hanging shower curtain effect.

The thing is, if you are currently a little over your fighting weight, clothes that fit more closely on the body are actually much more flattering than capacious volumes, especially if the larger items are clearly too big on your shoulders. It's all about proportion.

Even if you are seriously in the Mama Cass range of figures, baggy clothes are not necessarily more becoming. They don't hide your girth, they attract attention to it. And just as a sea monster looks more enormous swimming about in the briny depths, your undefined body mass will appear greater beneath the tent-like folds.

Really, it's much better to just come out and declare 'This is my shape, I have a little poodge issue right now, so deal with it, OK?' and wear clothes that upholster your girth, rather than swamp it. Not in skin-tight, shiny spandex, but in clothes that simply fit you.

So in this spirit, I'll be taking my Splendid top back and changing it for a Medium. Hurrah.

Fashion physics

Maybe I should have listened more in physics at school, but throughout my school years it was my class of most suffering. Even maths was more fathomable, Latin endings a mere irritation by comparison.

The only thing that was bearable about Double Physics (Thursday afternoon – I will never forget it) was when Mr Boland, the lovely chemistry teacher from the neighbouring lab, let his miniature Yorkshire terrier puppy – Tuppence – escape. A jet-propelled ball of toffee-coloured fluff would go charging round the physics benches, yapping. Oh, how we cheered. I always suspected he did it on purpose to lighten our days.

Apart from that, I cannot remember a single thing about those lessons, not even the name of the teacher, who might as well have been speaking in Klingon, for all I could make of it.

Anyway, this has all come back recently as I have only just realised that physics has an impact on clothing.

Perhaps if our Klingon teacher had mentioned the effect

of combining fabrics with a nap, or pile, with knits in one outfit (Alderson's Theorem), my brain might have shifted out of standby for a moment and downloaded something. But oh no, he was far too interested in cogs and levers to tell us anything really useful.

Anyway, so I don't really understand how it happens, but if you combine as above – say, a pair of crushed velvet pants with a long-line cashmere jumper – the knit top will sort of walk up the velvet and gather at your waist in a most unattractive fashion. It's a kind of living Velcro arrangement and can quite ruin your evening, as I found out the hard way.

The reverse syndrome involves shaved legs and hosiery; the tights walk down the stubbly hairs to gather in Nora Batty pools at your ankles.

Another horrible experience I have had due to the inadequate teaching of fashion physics at my school is of wearing certain kinds of unlined skirts over tights. Some kind of friction between the two fabrics – and it doesn't always happen – causes the skirt to become balled up between the legs, dhoti-style, as you walk. This is extremely humiliating.

Of course, the way to be certain these things won't happen is always to wear a slip beneath your skirt, but petticoats cause all kinds of problems of their own, particularly that style of silky jersey slip which is usually bought to wear underneath sheer evening wear.

These have a strange way of growing from the shoulder straps as you wear them, so that they sit ever lower on your upper torso, to the point where I have looked down at many a black-tie dinner to see my bra on full view through my top, with the slip slung hammock-like beneath it. Mortifying. You spend the rest of the evening putting your hand down your cleavage to yank it up, which must look very unusual, if not borderline psychotic.

I have taken a certain comfort recently in knowing that this doesn't affect only me. A quick camera pan to an audience member at a recent awards ceremony broadcast (think it was the BAFTAs) revealed a woman sitting in her special red-carpet outfit, quite unaware that millions were scoping her rather ordinary bra while her slip took a holiday somewhere around her waist.

Less embarrassing, but extremely irritating over the hours of a day, is a strange thing that happens involving the two silver bangles I always wear on my right wrist and lightweight knit tops. With knits of a certain gauge, the sleeve gets caught between the bangles and they somehow haul it down, fire-bucket chain style, so it gets longer and longer until it sticks out of the bottom of my jacket sleeve, like a little boy wearing a he'll-grow-into-it school uniform. Drives me nuts.

Equally annoying are the trousers of just the right length to get caught on the top of ankle boots when you walk, creating an instant Star Trek look.

So could physics have saved me from all these indignities?

peDoghQo' *

---

* Klingon for 'Don't be silly.' Sourced from the Klingon Language Institute: www.kli.org

Laundry love

It has often been said that food is love, but don't you think that laundry is love too? This thought came to me this morning as I handwashed the tiny pink cashmere cardigan a generous friend gave my daughter Peggy when she was born.

Using a special cashmere 'shampoo', I washed that little cardie with the care of a curator cleaning an unbroken glass found in a newly discovered Roman villa. First I gently squeezed the detergent bubbles through the knit, as taught by my mother, never rubbing or scrubbing, but paying particular attention to the front, where dried milk and banana porridge lurked, and to the cuffs, which had seen some serious chewing action. Then, after several progressively cooler rinses (to settle the fibres) and a spin, I put it carefully out to dry, lying flat on a towel, near – but not too near – a radiator.

Later on I anticipate pressing it, using a just-warm iron and my special pressing mesh designed for protecting woollies. Then I will put it away in Peggy's drawer with a lavender bag snuggled next to it.

Next time I dress her in it, the scent of the cashmere shampoo and the lavender will perfume our morning. And I will smell it again every time I kiss her soft little neck, which is quite often as the day goes on.

I will enjoy every step of that process, which is why, while I joyously share all the household tasks and childcare evenly with my husband (thank you Emmeline, Germaine, Gloria, et al, it was all worth it), I jealously guard my right to do the washing. This is quite selfish, really, as I love doing it, yet am still able to claim it as a share of my work points, against which he is obliged to take out the garbage, vacuum the stairs and wash the kitchen floor.

Rather as some men extravagantly take over the cooking, thus absolving themselves of all responsibility for other, less rewarding chores. Such as scrubbing the terracotta-hard fresh ricotta and spinach lasagne off the baking tray, or balancing the household budget after forays into bravura lobster dishes and $35 organic chickens.

While certainly a vast improvement from the 'where's my dinner?' Neanderthal, that kind of display cooking can demand loud praise of the 'you're-so-lucky, isn't Trevor wonderful?' variety, while Trevor beams smugly, pops open another bottle of vintage shiraz and claims spiritual kinship with Neil Perry. ('It's all in your stock, mate.')

Laundry is a quieter pleasure. The hobby laundress has more in common with the brownies; it's love by stealth. Everyone in the house always has clean socks and undies, which appear, neatly paired and folded, just where they expect them to be. They never really think about how they got there, but at a subconscious level it makes them all feel happier in their lives. A deep-seated sense that all's right with the world can be created just by someone happily keeping on top of the washing.

I'm so keen on it all that I even voluntarily use washable nappies for Peggy. Mind you, they are a lot more fun than they used to be. Forget those dreadful old terry towelling things – she has leopard-print nappies, shaped like little loincloths, that snap on and off with poppers. Sweaty plastic pants have been replaced by equally ergonomic and fashionable breathable microfibre wraps that close with Velcro.

What started out as an investigation of a more environmentally tolerable alternative to disposable nappies turned into a fabulous shopportunity. And the washing of them (a cinch – you just flush any unpleasantness down the loo, chuck them in a lidded bucket to soak and throw the whole lot into the washer at the end of the day), is another way of showing my love for her.

Which is clearly bred in the bone. When my mum comes to stay she still does my hand washing.

Revert to type

Well, I've looked right through John Betjeman's* *Collected Poems*, but I still can't find the one I'm looking for. It's driving me nuts. I read it years ago and a line from it lodged in my brain and I really need to read it again.

It was one of his poems about a young woman from the Home Counties – a bit of a theme of his. (He clearly had a thing about women in 'slacks'.) Anyway, this one went up to London – I think she went to art college – and had a bit of a bohemian time. Bearded men in chunky jumpers, coffee bars, fishnet stockings – that kind of 1950s caper. Sort of Miss Joan Hunter Dunn's arty little sister. But the point of it was that in the end she goes back to Surrey and marries a suitable boy. 'They always revert to type' is the line that haunts me.

* After publication I was besieged with emails from *Good Weekend* readers reminding me that the line in question was actually by the Australian poet Peter Porter and not by Betjeman at all. Oops.

It's such a casually damning little phrase and it came back to me like a punch to the jaw the other night. At the time, I was standing in my bathroom, with heated rollers in my hair, putting on my false eyelashes. Rigging myself up like a three-shows-nightly drag queen, for an event in a dodgy venue in a small provincial town.

Omigod, I thought, looking at my garish reflection, as I realised I used to do exactly the same thing twenty-five years ago, when I first started going out. To dodgy venues in another small provincial town.

OK, so this wasn't quite such a parochial outing. My friend Steve was putting on his cabaret show (Robbie Williams is just one of his fans), with a bunch of musicians who tour with big-name artistes, but just coincidentally happen to live near me the rest of the time.

Whereas the kind of thing I used to get dressed up for at seventeen involved unknown and never-to-be-known bands – featuring my friends – at whatever desperate local venue they could persuade to have them. But to me and my gang, they were still big nights.

In between has been a period of relative sophistication. Dressing with a degree of restraint and elegance for grown-up events in proper big cities, or more extravagantly for major big nights (the Cointreau Ball, legendary New York club Area, Andrew Logan's Alternative Miss World). But now, I realise that to all intents, I'm right back where I started from.

Like the man said: 'They always revert to type . . .' And

I suppose my type must be small-town girl with big ideas. Certainly big hair. The realisation put a bit of a dampener on the proceedings, which up to that point I had been thoroughly enjoying, because — just as when I was sixteen — creating the 'look' was often the best part of the night for me.

Now I wondered whether it wasn't a bit tragic for a woman of my age to be getting into the Carmen rollers and the false eyelashes. Another reference shot into my head: the woman in *Midnight Cowboy* who picks up Jon Voight. Closely followed by Terence Stamp in *The Adventures of Priscilla, Queen of the Desert*.

For a moment there, I was tempted to scrub it all off, pull my hair back into a ponytail and abandon the little black dress and sequinned shrug for jeans. Or even stay in. But I did neither, because in the end I decided it would be sadder to give in to middle age and the sofa than to go out wearing a big look in a small town.

So that's the lesson here. If we do all, inevitably, revert to type, the thing is to acknowledge the type you are, and learn to love it. To quote another great line: I am what I am.

Push out the olive boat

I have just been indulging in one of my favourite vices – flicking through a gorgeous poncy catalogue with no intention of buying anything.

This particular piece of shopping porn was from a high-end cookware emporium and I was happily contemplating the perfect liquidiser and those genius salad spinners where you just have to press the knob, when my eye was caught by the 'Olive Boat'. This is possibly the most stupid thing I have ever encountered.

It's a long, thin French porcelain, er, thingy, specially designed to hold about twenty olives – in a neat row, like Viking oarsmen. Yours for just $30!

In case you are concerned you might not get enough use from it for olives, it says in the helpful caption: 'Also a great way to display and serve quails' eggs, cherry tomatoes, or radishes.'

Now, the word 'display' does leap out of that sentence as particularly bollocks-y, but I would be hypocritical if I didn't admit that I do care quite a bit about having things look nice around my house. And a certain awareness of the 'display' of mundane things is all part of that.

In the kitchen, for example, I like to store my lemons in a nice yellow bowl I bought in a French supermarket. It looks sunny and gay and they're always handy when I want to make a salad dressing. Or a large drink.

When I have friends over for said libations, I enjoy serving olives in the fabulous 1950s art pottery soup bowls I bought in an antiques emporium in the Blue Mountains. They are all different colours with contrasting glazes on the inside and extremely pleasing to the eye. So is a plump pile of juicy olives tumbled into them.

But 'displaying' your olives or radishes in a serried line is another thing entirely. You'd have to place each one into the olive/radish/quail egg/cheese football boat with nimble little fingers. I feel itchy just thinking about it.

There wouldn't be much to go round, either. If I came to your house for a cocktail and you presented me with twenty olives in a row like that, I'd be tempted to funnel the lot straight down my gullet in one movement, head back, like a force-fed goose.

And think what you'd have to do to a bunch of radishes to make them look neat enough for the French porcelain boat. You'd have to give each one a ritual circumcision, which is a damn shame as radishes in the raw have such wonderful bushy green leaves and whiskery curly ends. I have been known to wash a few bunches and use them as a centrepiece on a dinner table, with saucers of sea salt and butter strewn about. Decorations you can break off and eat are great fun.

Anyway, after meeting Miss Olive Boat, I was on high alert for other things to despise in the catalogue. It wasn't hard when you can buy a packet of twenty paper 'cheese leaves' for $24 (I didn't know cheese grew on trees, did you?), or an asparagus cooking pot for $100, or a feather duster for nearly the same amount. I was also struck by a wooden bread 'crock' for $250. Crock is the right word for it.

Outraged as I am by these prices, this is not to say I am against paying out big for the best cooking utensils. Au contraire, I'm all for it. It was a struggle to buy two Le Creuset casseroles when I was twenty-three, but I'm still using them today. More recently I've bought the best roasting pans I could find – wonderful heavy French things – and my baked chook has been elevated to a new sphere as a result. Gravy practically makes itself in them.

Likewise, I'm all for having the right vessel for the job. You need a soufflé dish to make a soufflé and ramekins and a blowtorch to make proper crème brûlée. But nobody ever needed an olive boat.

Clothing compatibility

There are certain genres of clothing I will never be able to wear. This – for once – has nothing to do with being middle-youthed, with knees and upper arms well past their sell-by dates. I am talking about garments that have never suited me and never will. We are just not compatible.

It's mainly to do with physical proportions. Take, for example, the swirling gypsy skirt. I have always longed to wear one of those. I yearned to swish around in one in 1974 – I was always trying them on in shops and even bought a couple, which I never wore – and in more recent times the desire has been rekindled by the gorgeous clothes of Brisbane-based label Easton Pearson, who seem to specialise in ravishing circular skirts.

Pam Easton and Lydia Pearson, the designers behind the label, wear their own clothes all the time and look totally fabuloso in them. Every time I see them, I long to be wearing a gypsy skirt myself, especially with a pair of divine flat boots, the way they do, but I know it cannot be. Put one of those heavenly skirts on and I would look like Humpty Dumpty in drag.

It's partly because I'm hugely a short arse, of course, but it's not just that. Lydia is not particularly tall either, but she looks wonderful in her skirts because she is so petite, particularly in the upper body. They are both really *neat* up there and that is the crucial thing, plus they both go in at the waist, which is the essential counterpoint to a big skirt.

I, on the other hand, have broad swimmers' shoulders, an uncontrollable bosom and no waist. Oh yeah, I've got a small bottom and really small hips, but they don't do much for me under a gypsy skirt. In fact, you need a bit of hip jut to create a frame for the skirt to sit on. Almost like a built-in crinoline.

But although proportions are a large part of it, they are not the only reason why a circular skirt will never be mine. Although I long to stride around Paris during the shows, as Pam and Lydia do, in those wonderfully romantic clothes, I know it just isn't my look. I may *feel* romantic – and it's hard not to, in Paris in February, with mist over the Seine and the Louvre rising up before you – but I know it's not how I come over.

I'm a practical, pragmatic, tailoring girl. By staying true to myself, on a good day, I can pull off Fashionista Princess, and at the weekend I am right across Quality Blonde Smart Casual. Those are the looks for me; I was born that way. It's almost like having a clothes star sign.

So this is how, with age and experience, I have given up raging against my fashion fate. I know the styling star I was born under and I have accepted it – more than that – I have embraced it.

Take, for example, another garment I shall never again attempt to wear: the palazzo pant. I think they are so elegant, so Coco Chanel-ish. I love the idea of gliding around in a pair with a big hat and huge black sunnies, but it's not to be. Palazzo pants make me look like Danny de Vito.

It must be my lack of height again, but my girlfriend Jo, who is only about three inches taller than me, looks genius in palazzos. I can't tell you the times I have walked beside her on a summer day, grinding my teeth and muttering, as she strode out in a pair of flowing white linen pants and some Manolo slides, swinging a Provençal basket. Grrrrrr.

But then, Jo says she can't wear jeans. I feel like I was born in jeans and always have. So her clothing star sign is Palazzos and mine is Denim. I can live with that.

Ageing beautifully

I get enough shocks with regards to ageing when I look in the mirror these days, but I have recently experienced another kind of reflection of the passing years, which is the effect of passing time on the faces of old friends.

And old is the operative word here. It is so weird catching sight of someone you first met in the full bloom of youth and seeing a middle-aged person looking back at you. Especially when you know they are experiencing the same time warp when they look at you.

This really struck me the other week, when I bumped into a former acquaintance I hadn't seen for several years. In the intervening time she had aged so dramatically, I hope I didn't gasp when I saw her. As I've mentioned before, it's a term I really dislike, but I couldn't help feeling she had 'let herself go'.

She'd gained loads of weight, was dressed scruffily – where she used to be ultra-chic – and her once-glossy hair was a mess of wild grey strands. Despite the lines that had formed on it, her exquisitely pretty face was the same, but I wondered whether I would have been able to see it through all the distracting accoutrements of age, if I hadn't known it was there.

And that was what made this unexpected rendezvous particularly striking – this woman was unusually beautiful in her youth. She had an exotic loveliness that hypnotised men. Heads really would swivel, cartoon-style, as she walked down the street, and I have seen blokes rendered almost speechless by her at first meeting.

It wasn't a raw sex appeal, charisma thing, so much as the sheer perfection of her features that used to strike them dumb. She was almost impossibly pretty and had what you might call a very pretty figure, too. She was never a model, but that beautiful visage appeared in several arty books, as successive photographers and artists sought to capture it.

My own first husband – a painter himself – was one of them. He was fascinated by her face and while I don't think he ever thought of hitting on her, he always treated her in a special way, with a kind of fond reverence. All of which made it hard for the insecure, youthful me ever to feel easy in her company. Not that I didn't like her; I really did. She was good fun, interesting to talk to and never anything but lovely to me, but I always felt awkward – not to mention ugly – around her.

And I have to admit that when confronted by the aged version, all that unease was gone. For the first time I felt I was interacting with her as an equal and was able to enjoy her warm, up-beat personality without her beauty getting in the way.

But the really interesting thing that struck me was that I had never seen her happier. When I'd first known her, she was living the London high life, out on the town, famous boyfriends, designer gear, exotic holidays, a permanent suntan, the works.

But while she appeared to have the lifestyle to which we were all supposed to aspire, she never quite seemed comfortable in it. I always felt there was a stone in her shoe.

Now she's living in the country, with her not-famous husband and growing family, not glamorous at all, and that stone is definitely gone. She seemed as at ease with herself as I finally was in her company.

And even beyond the satisfaction of raising some great kids – she had them with her – I felt she was relieved to have put the beauty behind her. I suppose that beauty on that level must carry the responsibility that goes with all inherited privilege, and it was as though she had set it aside like a heavy weight.

It's good to know that growing old has some upsides, isn't it?

White hot

I have recently been seen in public carrying a white handbag. I wasn't carrying it for a friend, to the dump, or for a dare, which are just about the only circumstances I would have been seen holding such an object until about two weeks ago. I was carrying it with pride, even a certain swagger. I love my white handbag. It's so cool.

I can hardly begin to describe what a shift in attitude this represents. Up until my recent conversion I didn't just dislike white handbags, the way I dislike, for example, the music of Gilbert and Sullivan, the writing of Jeffrey Archer and the food of Colonel Saunders. I loathed them. I felt strongly about them.

It wasn't even just that I considered them daggy, like a fleece zip top worn in the CBD. Or tasteless and tacky, like sheer lace trousers. I objected to white handbags at a deep moral level. I'm not quite sure why, but to me they have always been something that right-minded adults didn't carry about. They were beyond the pale (whatever that is).

I voiced this point of view quite a while ago and somebody wrote to me and asked if she couldn't carry a white handbag, what was she supposed to put with her white shoes? My instinctive reply would have been: do you really need your handbag on a tennis court? But of course I was much more polite: 'Match your bag with the rest of your outfit, or if wearing an all-white ensemble, navy, red, or camel would all look very chic – just not black.'

Which was very restrained considering I feel exactly the same way about white shoes as I used to feel about white handbags. Beauty queens – and everything those two words stand for.

I still don't quite understand what has changed my mind so radically, although Miuccia Prada had something to do with it, as usual. Quite a while ago her company started pushing the white bag as its new anchor accessory and I was horrified. What a waste of beautiful leather, I hufflepuffed, as people I thought had more taste paraded shamelessly around with small white pigskin bags over their shoulders, worked back with chic winter tailoring.

I thought they'd lost their reason in some kind of brainless mass obedience to any edict from the Mighty Miuccia (the Big Sister of high fashion), until suddenly – just the other week – I realised they had been right all along. White bags can be really chic – especially when worn in unexpected combinations. It's precisely the surprise element that makes them work.

In my previous mindset I might have said that I could

have countenanced a white canvas bag for the beach, but the exact thing I like about my new white leather shoulder bag is wearing it in the city. It just took a bit longer for me to get my eye in to the look than it did my more fashion-prescient colleagues.

But I would like to think that my conversion to the white bag is about more than them simply becoming highly trendy. Brazenly wearing something which I now realise I had been indoctrinated *from childhood* into thinking was a total fashion no-no feels thrillingly wicked.

Although I know I wasn't on the first wagon train with this trend, I still feel like a fairly early uptaker and it's quite a kick. Rather like wearing the outrageous New Look in 1941 must have been, or the first miniskirts in the 1960s. In fact, the last time I had a frisson like this would have been when I made my debut in Seditionaries bondage pants in 1977.

And things have moved on so much since then, with once-shocking notions such as topless sunbathing, lady tattoos, piercing, bare midriffs and visible bras and G-strings all becoming everyday sights, that there aren't many fashion taboos left to flout.

Reckon I'll be in white high heels by Christmas.

New carpet blues

As I blotted – not scrubbed – the spilled tea on the hall carpet with a clean, damp – not soaking wet – undyed dishcloth (those blue or yellow ones can transfer their colour and just make things worse), I wondered whether I had fulfilled that most patronising of Wilde-isms and turned into my mother.

Because apart from the constantly lost spectacles and the cries of 'Is it hot in here, or is it me?', one of the most vivid images I have of my mama is her on all fours, blotting stains from carpets. And quickly, mind! Before they set! The first few minutes after a spill are crucial, you see.

Many's the time I have seen her breaking land speed records, weaving through the crowd at one of her parties, holding a soda siphon aloft. Fizzy water is marvellous for carpet stains. And if it was red wine, she'd have the salt in the other hand.

Now she has gone high-tech and has a wonderspray guaranteed to zap all stains dead with just a few squirts. The only problem is that it gives off such pungent chemical fumes

I think it could have the same effect on small mammals, if not humans. And it probably has a half-life roughly equivalent to nuclear waste.

There was a whole area of her sitting room that we had to practically cordon off with HazChem tape after a Christmas wine spill, the wafts smelled so toxic. Couldn't see where the claret had gone over, though. Oh no. Gone.

The thing is, I am now wondering whether to purchase one of these deadly chemical stain sprays myself. If I'd had it to hand I wouldn't be constantly confronted by the memory of the day I left a full mug of tea on the floor at the top of the kitchen staircase, when I was rushing back down to answer the phone, and my husband, quite forgivably, kicked it down the stairs.

I got most of it off the flat treads of the steps, but despite an hour or so of dabbing and blotting, you can still clearly see the tannin trail down the vertical part of one of the stairs. It's driving me tonto. As is the small round mystery mark on the landing outside the bedroom. What is it? And what *bastard* put it there?

Now it could be simple genetics that has turned me, with age, into a combination of Hyacinth Bucket and Howard Hughes, but I actually think it is simpler (and less insulting to my mother) than that. It's having new carpet.

I've never had this much new carpet before (halls and stairs, top to bottom) and certainly not such nice stuff. And, looking back, I remember it was having her first really nice carpet that turned my mum into the sprinter with the soda siphon.

At no time, while we were living in my childhood home, can I remember her racing to the kitchen for her stain-saver kit. There must have been carpets in that house, but I can't really remember them and they certainly weren't special enough to warrant the soda siphon. I think they came with the house and four children were left to do pretty much what they wanted with them.

But when we all left home and my parents moved, they carpeted the new place throughout in 100 per cent wool carpet. In pale cream. That was when stainmania began and despite another move, to a house where she put in more sensible carpet, it hasn't left her.

I think it must be something to do with choosing the carpet yourself, paying for it (ouch), and then the utter gorgeousness of it that brings this condition on.

So if I ever have new carpet again, I'm going to throw a mug of tea down the stairs on the first day and get over it.

Starting over

I recently had one of those twice-yearly change-of-season sort-outs. You know, when you go through all your summer clothes, marvel at why you bought most of them, sigh over a few tired old faithfuls, wonder how the rest ever fitted you – and then throw just a very small bag of them into a clothing bin?

This was a particularly thorough cull, though, long overdue, and I went through everything – undies, swimwear, shoes, nighties, accessories, even hangers – with a seriously critical and pragmatic eye. God, I'm bored with it all. What a lot of old junk most of it is.

It may not start out as junk, but clothing inevitably turns into it with wear and tear. Even your investment pieces conk out eventually. I sent my beloved Helmut Lang suit off to charity shop land last week, so if you see it, say hello (and advance apologies to anyone who seizes upon the jacket only to find that the trousers have been mutilated to fit my unusually stunted legs).

But while I was sad to ditch something that had been so useful and esteem-enhancing in its time, the things that depressed me the most during this biannual audit were the *nearly* great pieces.

I've got a particular little section in my wardrobe of *quite* good jackets that I've never worn much. They really should go, but I just can't bring myself to hurl things that still look box-fresh. Even though every time I look at them they are a reminder of a small failure of judgement, or of those days when you just have to buy something, even though you know it's not quite right.

So there I was once again looking at the saggy black 'shirt' jacket from Paris and the shapely black DKNY jacket with the really annoying two-way zip and I thought – what if I just threw it all out? All of it. Even the sock collection and the archaeological dig of underpants. Wouldn't it secretly be a relief?

Take the socks as an example. I've got loads of socks, of various vintages, most of them seriously on the dingy side. Mindful of this, I bought a whole new hosiery wardrobe when I was in Milan recently (they have wonderful shops for things like that there). With ten smart new pairs I really could chuck all the rest out. But I haven't, because it seems 'wasteful'.

It's the same with undies – why don't I just bin all the grey whites and the charcoal once-blacks that used to be great and buy seven new pairs in each colour? Wouldn't it be a lovely fresh start?

And why stop there? Couldn't I really just throw it all out? Of course you would want to keep a small core of recently purchased, current favourite pieces – ie the ones I actually wear – but the rest really could go, couldn't they?

Occasionally a garment has a comeback to rival Tony Bennett's, but it's so rare, it's hardly worth keeping the wardrobe in the spare room full of clapped-out old clobber for.

Imagine, by contrast, the joy of opening a wardrobe that wasn't stuffed and overflowing, where you could see everything and know how it worked together.

It would make getting dressed easier, it would make packing easier, and it would make staying tidy easier – three things that exercise a lot of my energy over a year.

Imagine also, once you had cleared your space of all the dross and guilt pieces, the fun you could have filling it up again.

Style swap

How gripping is that TV show *Wife Swap*? I find it fascinating. Mind you, I'm a total sucker for all those reality lifestyle programmes. If only they'd combine them all into one. *Dirty Holiday Home DIY Decorating Disaster Husband Swap Idol* would be perfection.

It would be about a couple swapping partners and then going to find their dream holiday home at the perfect price in the best location, location, location. Then they would have just one day to renovate, while losing two stone, getting a new fashion look, showing how filthy their lavvies are and cutting a single. And we, the viewers, would get to vote them off while they were doing it.

Anyway, that's just my little fantasy, but I did once have a mini-adventure of my own along the life swap line, when I was very young and silly. I was on holiday in Greece with some of my best uni gal pals. One of them, Jane, is just about the only person I know who is even shorter than me, with the same silly dolly-size feet. One night this gave us an idea.

We were sharing a 'cabana' (grass hut) and as we were getting dressed for 'dinner' (binge drinking) we decided to swap clothes for a laugh, to see if anyone noticed.

This was pretty funny because then — as now — I was a bit of a op-shopping city-slicker fashion victim and Jane is your classic Pommie Sloane Ranger. Back then, in 1985, she dressed like Diana Spencer, when she was still Diana Spencer. Jane even wore her string of pearls on the beach.

But that night she ended up wearing a black-and-white stripy singlet (like I said, it was 1985), with a black miniskirt, a black silk vintage pyjama jacket with white piping, and an armful of Nancy Cunard bangles. And I wore her drop-waisted pastel floral dress with *puff* sleeves and a Peter Pan collar, with ballerina pumps. Really.

I probably wouldn't have remembered the details quite so clearly, but I still have a photo of us taken outside our hut that night. Looking at it again now, I see we are even standing in each other's characteristic postures. I have my feet turned out at ten to two, like a ballet dancer, which is the way all Sloanes stand, for some reason. And Jane is standing like Henry VIII, with legs firmly planted, which seems, unfortunately, to be the way I stand.

Our friends nearly lost it when they saw us. They just couldn't believe how different we looked and they also pointed out that in a funny kind of way we actually looked better in each other's clothes than we did in our own. Jane is a ravishing brunette dusky maiden and she looked seriously great in my outfit, and I have to say — looking at this here photo – I was a passable English rose in that godawful frock. It was so weird.

The funny thing was, neither of us really behaved any differently that night, because while we dressed so differently, we were pretty similar in most ways, sharing a fondness for a white wine, a disco dance and a crude one-liner. (We still do; we're still mates.)

But while I didn't start behaving like a demure finishing-school debutante, I did have a glimpse of a different life in that outfit, because of the way people reacted to me. They were nicer. Sometimes I think life might have been easier as an English rose than it has been as a Darth Vader fashion victim.

But the crunch came when it was time to hit the dance floor. I just couldn't dance in that dress. I had to go back to the hut and put something black on. So life in florals might have been a less bumpy ride than it can be in urban fastwear, but it wouldn't have been nearly as much fun.

Saving string

A sense of dread gripped me as I read the 'letter to parents' on the nursery noticeboard. 'Think Before You Throw It!' was the heading, followed by these terrible words: 'Please save your loo-roll and paper-towel centres, yoghurt pots, egg boxes, washing-up liquid bottles, wrapping paper and ribbon for our craft projects. You'll be amazed what we will do with them!'

They would be amazed if they knew what an apparently harmless request like that could do to me. By the next day my utility room was less of a laundry and more of a sorting office. Different carrier bags were festooned from an array of hooks, for maximum filing efficiency, on the following lines: cardboard cylinders, assorted; egg cartons, various; yoghurt pots, large and small; miscellaneous items with possible craft potential.

The reason I had managed to amass such an impressive collection so quickly was that I was able to repossess many of the items instantly from my large recyling area, just to get the crafts materials projects off to an encouraging start. Did I also slightly go round the bins in the house looking for other possible items? Well, maybe I did.

Certainly when I worked in the *Sydney Morning Herald* offices, I used to go through my colleagues' bins at night, re-directing all the paper they had carelessly thrown into the garbage into the paper-recycling bins, and the padded envelopes under my own desk for future use.

I've got quite a collection of padded envelopes now in my home office. It's about the size of a large sheep. And sometimes I can hardly get to my desk for the paper-recycling system, which runs as follows:

Printed both sides: recycle now. Printed one side: use other side for printing rough work, then recycle. Printed one side, but crinkled: make into shopping list pad, or toddler art pad, with bulldog clip.

Then there are the great termite mounds of magazines that I still need to go through for charming pictures of animals for the collage I am going to do on my daughter's playroom wall. One year. A large area on the bookcase behind me is taken up by my collection of used stamps, which I am gathering for charity.

This was another endeavour that saw me fossicking in *Sydney Morning Herald* waste bins after everyone else had gone home. I used to bring them back from all the invitation envelopes I received in Milan and Paris for the fashion shows, too. And I've got my mother saving them for me. In fact, I would probably run across a five-lane highway at

8 am on a Monday morning to save one franked stamp from going to waste.

And that is what all this neurotic behaviour is about – I really can't stand waste. Lord knows, I'm not tight with a dollar, it's not that I wouldn't shell out for a new padded envelope, it just seems wrong to crack open a fresh one, when an old stager could do another turn.

Indeed, some of my envelopes have been round the world several times, back and forth between me and like-minded hoarders on other continents, so at least I know I am not alone in this obsessive-compulsive recycling.

Just the other night a friend told me that she is still incapable of chucking out a loo-roll middle that could be craftily fashioned into a spaceship, a snake, or a sausage dog – and her daughter is twenty-five.

I take comfort in the belief that this neurosis is fundamentally an environmental issue for my age group. Our generation certainly doesn't have the war as an excuse – unlike the elderly gentleman I once heard about, who had been left so anxious about scarcity by living through the Second World War that he had a box in his attic labelled: 'String, too short to use.'

But then again, couldn't it have made charming fur for a loo-roll-inside shaggy dog? I might have to start another carrier bag . . .

Getting branded

I've got a tat. As in a tattoo. Just like that, on a whim, I went and logged into one of the style crazes I have despised most in the past ten years.

I hate tattoos. Whenever I look at my little girl's perfect skin I pray to the fashion gods that she won't ever besmirch it with one of these foul blemishes, and now I've got one.

Of course, they can look great on smooth young skin, especially brown skin that is tightly spread over taut muscle, but I remember all too clearly what my grandfather's arms looked like when he was in his seventies and the tattoos he'd done himself in the trenches during the First World War were blurred blue smudges on his crepey skin.

It was not a good look, but as he was fond of joking, at the time he did them, with the end of his bayonet and some India ink, he didn't expect to live another day, let alone another fifty-eight years, so he wasn't really looking at the long-term picture. So that was his excuse, but why have I gone and done it? For laughs, really.

I'm in New York at the moment (omigod, it's the best place on earth, it's been five years and I'd almost forgotten) and it just happens to be Pride this weekend, which is their version of Mardi Gras, with the big parade and everything, and I just got swept up by it all. One minute I was walking along Eighth Street, on my way to get a good parade pozzie, the next I was in the tattoo shop getting my mark made.

I think it was partly wanting to join in, show solidarity and be part of the gang, because everyone I was passing seemed to have tattoos and I felt rather left out. And I suppose it was also an act of bravado to make a middle-aged woman feel a bit young and reckless, as I used to be for real when I hung out in New York in the 1980s.

I hope it ends better than my last such desperate expression of youthful rebellion, when I had the gristly bit of my left ear pierced, just before my thirty-fifth birthday. That outing led to a week in hospital on turbo-charged pain-killers and an antibiotic drip, a missed holiday and an ear that now sticks out rather more than the other.

So do you want to know what I had? If I had gorgeous upper arms I would have had one of those Maori bicep rings, but I don't, so I went for something smaller, but still in that location. Ankles are all very well, but I've always felt the bicep was the classic tattoo spot. I like the retro associations of 1950s bad boys with their T-shirt sleeves rolled up, like the sexy one in *Grease*.

My first choice of design was the word 'Princess' topped off with a cheeky little tiara over the first letter, but the script wasn't quite camp enough, so I went for something more graphic – two entwined black Cs; that is, the Chanel logo.

I don't apologise for finding this intensely amusing. I also like the fact that not everyone will understand the reference, because I know all my friends will and mocking laughter will ensue. And even if people don't get the joke, it's an elegant symbol.

So that's me and my tat. I'm destined to be branded as a luxury goods item for the rest of my life. Well, no actually. For two weeks only. It's not a real tattoo; it's a pretend one done with black henna, but it will look fairly convincing while it lasts, and I intend to get maximum mileage surprising and horrifying friends and family with it when I get home.

Teenage dirtbags

I have been making a study of teenage boys. It was prompted by the arrival of a friend for dinner, who is the mother of a sixteen-year-old chap. She was in a state of shock. Her beloved son had turned overnight from her best pal into a foul beast.

'It's so awful,' she said, tears in her eyes. 'He used to get into bed with me and talk about poetry. Now he slams his bedroom door in my face.'

I really felt sorry for her, but I was able to offer a crumb of comfort: it won't last. I know this from my studies.

What I have recently observed in two young men I have known since they were just days old – a nephew and the son of a friend so dear he might as well be a nephew – is that boys do emerge from the adolescent horror period, just as girls do. The whole process just happens a little later. Girls seem to go into the tunnel at about thirteen and emerge at sweet sixteen, whereas boys go in at fifteen and come out at eighteen. From what I've seen, you could almost set your clock by it.

The processes are also different. I have described the girl version already as the Swan Moment, when a lumpy, bumpy, painful adolescent girl suddenly transforms into a beautiful young woman. With the boys it's not so much the ugly duckling as the Very Hungry Caterpillar. They certainly have appetites comparable to that voracious bug.

I couldn't believe it when I had a sixteen-year-old nephew to stay (who was so deep in the zone at the time, I had practically kidnapped him for a visit, to save my brother's sanity and possibly prevent a murder in the family). Man, could he eat. He could get through a whole packet of cereal at one meal. Gallons of milk disappeared. Fistfuls of pies.

So he was a Very Hungry Teenager, but the other similarity is the chrysalis stage. Whereas girls in the teen tunnel are gawky and awkward things who look as though they have been put together from some ill-matched spare parts, boys are simply monstrous. They really disappear entirely into their new personas. They usually have pimples, they adopt an unflattering (and usually unwashed) hairstyle and wear frightful baggy clothes – preferably the same ones every day. Plus trainers of terrifying fungal rottenness. Really they are just festering mounds of hormones. It's terrible to see. Especially when you have dandled them on your knees, when theirs were still dimpled.

And that's just their appearance. On top of that you have the stun-gun attitude to deal with, plus the incomprehensible caveman grunting that passes for speech and a universal terrible sniggering laugh. Which is why that

American cartoon *Beavis and Butthead*, about two appalling teenage heavy metal freaks, is so hilariously perfect. They're ugly. They have dreadful hair. They communicate entirely in grunts and sniggers. And their only interests are very loud, screeching guitars, humiliating each other, and breasts. It's practically a home video, it's so spot-on.

At one point my friend's son was turning into such a Butthead I was quite worried about him, but his aunt – who had observed the syndrome in three younger brothers – told me to keep the faith.

'One day he'll suddenly turn into Cary Grant,' she kept telling me. I didn't believe her – but it turns out she was right. Just a few weeks shy of his eighteenth birthday, he's cut off his dreadful curtain of filthy hair and done something serious about looking for a job. He's also delightful. 'Do come in for a cup of tea,' he said to me, the last time I gave him a lift home. I nearly fainted.

I'm delighted to say that the same transformation has taken place in my nephew, who is suddenly an extremely affable and handsome eighteen-year-old.

Beautiful butterflies, the pair of them.

Unshopping

Oh, you should see all the beautiful things I didn't buy today. Racks and racks of gorgeous clothes, shelves of shoes, swathes of scarves and massed ranks of other accessories; it's really a marvel what I didn't bring home.

After such a wonderful day spent scoping out two of London's leading fashion department stores floor by floor (Selfridges and Liberty & Co, which have both recently been fabulously upgraded), I have come to the conclusion that un-shopping is almost as much fun as the real thing.

In fact it's better, because you don't have the terrible post-buying depression to deal with the next day, when the euphoria wears off and you just feel incredibly guilty about wasting money on sparkly purple shoes when so many people in the world don't even have clean drinking water.

I have always thought that such unshopping is mid-way on a daydreaming scale between *Breakfast at Tiffany's*-style window shopping and that slightly creepy thing of trying on things you know you can't afford and have no intention of buying, which is a bit too *Talented Mr Ripley* for my liking.

All unshopping consists of is a completely harmless stroll through the store, picking up things to admire them, feeling fabric between your fingers, maybe slipping a foot into a tempting mule, or holding an earring up to your face. It can be enough just to turn a hanger on the rail for a better look at something. Even with such a brief encounter, that garment becomes a tiny part of your history.

For in that instant when you imagine how it would look on you, whether it would go with your other clothes, or fit into your lifestyle, you own it, in a way. In a moment you have all the pleasure of the garment without it turning into draggy baggage – metaphorical or actual. And you don't have to pay for it, either. It's like wine tasting – the experience without the consequences – and the most exquisite pleasures are always ephemeral.

Unshopping is also exactly the part of shopping that most men don't understand. My husband calls it 'daundering' when I waft about looking at things. His attitude is: we've come in here for a hairbrush, let's get the hairbrush and leave. He really cannot understand the point of looking at things you already know you are not going to buy. But to me, a really beautiful shop is almost like a museum; it is an edifying experience just looking at the lovely things, I don't need to take them home as well.

And it seems I'm not alone in my love of virtual shopping, because while I was cruising around Selfridges' designer salons having the best time fingering clothes I had last seen walking down catwalks in Paris, I noticed a newspaper cutting lying on a cash desk. Using my well-honed skills of reading upside-down (essential for any journalist), I saw that it was about a new breed of shopper that has emerged in London who are taking unshopping to another level. They called them 'shopping bulimics' in the article, and there were interviews with women who go on wild sprees in London's designer stores, then take all the gear back the next day.

It wasn't that naughty thing of buying something expensive, wearing it once and taking it back – these women hadn't done more than try it on in their bedrooms at home, if that; it was just the buzz of the buying part that they enjoyed.

I can see it would be fun to pretend to be Posh Spice for a day and go on a mad Gucci spree, but it's not very honest and it's not real unshopping. You know you are a proper unshopper when you can look a sales assistant in the eye and with all sincerity say, 'I'm just looking, thank you.'

Hanging out

Absolute waterfront. Seven beds, seven baths. His-and-hers walk-in closets. Teak decking. Family kitchen. Original floor-boards. Fifty-metre swimming pool. Sauna and spa. Gold dolphin taps. Guest cottage. Separate staff quarters. Jetty. Helipad. Private airstrip. Bigger than the house next door.

All that fantasy real estate stuff is well and good, but sometimes I think all I really need to be happy is a washing line.

There's nothing like hanging your wash on a line to dry, especially if there's a bit of sun – but not too much – and a brisk wind that will blow your clothes to the perfect stage of ironing-dry, faster than you would have thought possible.

And you'll have no need for those poncy lavender laundry rinses (although I confess I have quite a collection), because washing dried in the open air has a smell all its own – and fresh is the word for it.

It's not just the energy efficiency of it – wind power – that pleases me; it's also so much better for your clothes. Tumble-drying, or nuking, as I call it, actually strips fibres from them (that's what that hamster bed stuff you find in the lint-catcher is) and if you don't liberate the load at exactly the right moment, your clothes come out looking like one of those Iron Age chaps they find preserved in peat bogs. All nurdled.

When I dry my nighties on a washing line I don't need to iron them. The wind presses them and I can picture one of those swollen-cheeked cherubs you see on old maps as the West Wind, huffing and puffing until they are smooth.

I also find clothes hanging on a line aesthetically pleasing. I love the picturesque charm of those washing lines strung between buildings in Naples, which are as much fun to read as supermarket baskets.

Some nappies, a row of tiny undies lined up like ducklings, little shorts, a frilly best dress, a man's shirts and working trousers, four white blouses, a black dress and some aprons. One look at that and you can see the whole family, including grandma, heading off to Mass.

On one holiday in the south of France we stayed in a charming little stone farmhouse that had a washing line among the blossoming cherry trees. I took more photographs of our laundry hanging on that line – such a pleasing mix of white linen, blue and white stripes and the odd red sock – than I did of any of the local sights.

But even apart from the look of it and all those energy-saving advantages – that's my own energy, as well as the kind that falls under the Kyoto Protocol – there is, for me, another great advantage to line drying. I love the actual pegging-out bit.

There's something immensely grounding about going out into the garden and hanging out a basket of freshly washed clothes. Bringing it in again, folding it as you take it down – with the odd pause to bury your nose in the wonderful smell – and putting the pegs back into their special bag is truly satisfying. A job completed.

A friend of mine, from one of those fractured modern families, with about three stepmothers and all kinds of half-brothers and sisters, once told me he felt the same way about shelling peas, and that sitting in the garden one warm afternoon, shelling peas with his father in anticipation of a family dinner, is one of the happiest memories of his whole life.

I can relate to that. Because a particular morning hanging out washing in my mother's garden is one of mine. The sun shining down. Fresh air. Blackbirds hopping around on the lawn. God in his heaven and everything right with the world.

You really don't need that six-car garage. Sometimes the little things in life really are enough.

Thirty-five and under

A friend arrived for the weekend and brought me a beautiful vintage silk Liberty scarf as a hostess gift. She knows I have a 'thing' about old scarves, having witnessed me hyperventilating in junk shops as I uncover a cache of them in a nasty old cardboard box in a corner, so it was top gifting.

I immediately knotted it at my neck in the style of a Parisian artist and it entirely cheered up my smart casual ensemble. Its jewel colours in graphic blocks are perfect for this season and it instantly became my accessory du jour.

Later on I tied it around the crown of my navy canvas hat, which was another hit. The next day when we raided some garage sales together (she is equally afflicted with junkophilia), I knotted it around the handle of my junketeering mini-backpack (hands free for fossicking, notes and coins in separate zip pockets, it works a treat). Result, result, result.

My next move with the scarf was to tie it over my head in the haute hippy manner – low on the forehead, pointy ends tucked under the knot at the back, tied ends trailing. A little bit Woodstock, a little bit Celia Birtwell, it's a look I have worn from time to winsome time since I was about seventeen, and it has always made me feel somewhat up myself.

But when I checked myself out in the mirror today, the strains of Kate Bush singing 'Babushka' rang loudly in my ears. Not so much Talitha Getty as her distant relative, Kosovan Grandma.

So that is one styling manoeuvre I realise I will now have to put aside until I really am a grandma. This is a very great disappointment to me and yet another of the constant little reminders of ageing which make the process so irritating. All right, all right! I want to shout at the heavens, I've got the message, *tempus* flipping *fugit*, you don't have to keep rubbing it in!

Since this latest disappointment, I have been doing a mental catalogue of all the other sartorial quirks that are now lost to me as the mists of time roll over my life.

Many of them – such as micro-minis and backless dresses – cease to be viable because you no longer want to unleash large areas of naked flesh on the general public, lest a wobble or dimple should offend.

After a certain point, you also discover that an overabundance of vintage and op shop attire looks whimsical on the young, yet clownlike on the older person, and there are other garments, such as chunky cardigans, which look rule-breakingly cute on a younger gal, but instantly frumpy on her older sister.

So, with the intention of helping those who are still young to make the most of them while they can, I have assembled a list of Thirty Things to Wear Before You Are Thirty-five:

1. Hotpants.
2. Micro-miniskirts.
3. Skirts to the ankle as daywear.
4. A sarong as daywear.
5. Halternecks.
6. Anything strapless or backless.
7. Sheer.
8. Kooky hats which fit close to the head.
9. Vintage hats of any kind.
10. Hair ornaments.
11. Thigh boots.
12. Some wildly over-the-top high-fashion statements.
13. Something hilariously oversized, be it a sleeve, a pocket, a flight of buttons, a trouser leg, a bag or a platform shoe.
14. Something you have run up yourself in a couple of hours for a party.
15. Something milkmaid-ish.
16. Head-to-toe op shop ensembles.
17. Complete outfits from a particular era.
18. Very heavy feature make-up as a party look.
19. Very cheap clothes.
20. Vintage dresses.
21. Plaits and pigtails.

22. Triangle bikinis.
23. Crocheted dresses.
24. Stripy tights.
25. Patchwork.
26. Very kitsch op shop finds in terrifying man-made fibres.
27. Toe rings.
28. Ankle bracelets.
29. Really seriously drainpipe-y jeans.
30. Super low-rise jeans.

Wearing it out

I have long been an advocate of investment dressing – which is the principle of investing blocks of capital in a few superior garments which will last longer and make you happier more often, rather than making multiple smaller unit purchases of cheap tat you will have to sling after two outings. In short, the cost-per-wear system.

But recently I have become aware of another form of investment dressing and I'm feeling a bit conflicted about it. Mainly because it's not really investment dressing so much as investment clothes shopping.

Or more accurately, buying clothes as investments, the way some people buy fine wine or artworks. Not because they make their hearts beat faster, but because one day they will be worth more than they paid for them, so they'll be able to flog them off and pocket the profits. Gimme gimme gimme.

Of course, there is nothing wrong with making money. I'm all for it. If you don't make it, you can't spend it, I do get that, but it's the pointy-nosed attitude that goes with this particular way of making money that I don't like.

It's making something gorgeous and life-affirming into homework. Something you do because it's good for you, rather than because you just love it.

I loathe the idea of buying paintings specifically because they might increase in value. The only possible reason to buy a work of art is because you simply cannot live without it. Although at least with investment art you would have the daily pleasure of looking at the things before cashing in your chips.

And I do have a couple of wonderful elderly beatnik pals who have financed their twilight years by selling paintings and drawings acquired – simply for love – during their misspent youths. A Picasso drawing here, a Duncan Grant there, transmogrified into a roof, a garden, a comfortable chair and many a flagon of wine, although that was more luck than judgement.

The idea of buying wine as an investment, however – ie wine you never have any intention of drinking – makes me feel even iller than quaffing it all would. Laying wine down to age for your greater future supping pleasure is one thing, but laying it down to sell? What a self-limiting attitude to life.

And I feel exactly the same about taking this approach to clothing. Frocks as an investment possibility has emerged with the boom in vintage, and means that the old Ossie Clarke frock your auntie bought when she was a young thing in London in the 1970s is now worth a small fortune – but only if she wore it once and has kept it in acid-free tissue paper ever since.

If she had a good time in that dress and wore it to the Rainbow Room at Biba, San Lorenzo, Mr Chow and the after-premiere party of *Don't Look Now*, where she spilled red wine and vomit all over it, and then conceived your favourite cousin while still wearing it, it's virtually worthless. But it might mean rather a lot to her, don't you think?

This struck me on a personal level when I went to the Vivienne Westwood exhibition at the Victoria and Albert Museum in London recently and saw garments on display in it that I still own.

It was well weird, seeing the bondage pants and obscene T-shirts that I wore night and day for a couple of years displayed in great seriousness in glass cases at such an august institution. While mine lie like dead dogs in a trunk in my bedroom.

Had I never worn them, they would now be worth serious money on Ebay. But which would have given me greater pleasure in the long-term scheme of my life? Making a few hundred dollars to fritter away on middle-age comforts, or the joy of being nineteen and wearing the scariest coolest clothes on earth?

No contest.

Also by Maggie Alderson

Handbag Heaven

Maggie Alderson is a firm believer in heaven – Handbag Heaven, that is. Why else would finding a vintage Kelly bag seem like a blessing and resisting that Jamin Puech bag feel so hellish?

In this witty and irreverent book Maggie Alderson guides you through not only the perils of shopping but also everyday life, explaining among other things why even the smallest clothing purchase is a major life decision, and why Buddha was right when he said 'the root of all suffering is desire' . . . especially when it comes to Ricky Martin.

Open up Alderson's bag of goodies to find out about fashion, beauty myths, her theory of shopping relativity, hair, and cockroaches (ahem). No subject is off limits and no bag remains unturned.

Shoe Money

Have you ever wondered why . . .

- Even the truly stylish find it hard to do smart casual?
- All men look like James Bond in dinner jackets?
- All four-year-old girls are obsessed with pink?
- Fashionable people always wear black?
- Blondes have less fun?
- Some people will spend $6,000 on a handbag?

This book will explain all of these mysteries and many more.

And even if you've never pondered any of these issues, Maggie Alderson will amuse and entertain you with her finely tuned observations about everything from global style icons to when to wear that perfect red dress – with the leopardskin shoes, of course.

Australia's wittiest fashion and lifestyle commentator delivers a delightful bundle of wicked charm.

Cents and Sensibility

Stella Fain has a rule for men she likes: Make them wait . . . But the gorgeous Jay proves an exception to the rule when he bowls Stella off her Prada wedges at a press junket on the Cote d'Azur.

He might seem to have everything going for him, but Stella is about to realise that while jetset lifestyles can be fabulous, her career as a journalist isn't something she wants to jeopardise for any man, no matter how filthy-rich or gorgeous.

And then there's her father – a six-times-married prime slice of Alpha Male with a grudge against inherited wealth . . . and Jay.

There's no denying money makes the world go round and diamonds are a girl's best friend, but they don't make the path to love any easier to tread – with or without the Prada wedges.

Handbags and Gladrags

As far as fashion stylist Emily Pointer is concerned, life is perfect. She's a natural blonde and a tall size 10, she travels the world for work and she gets 30 per cent discount at Prada.

So surely a night of wild sex with a hunky Australian photographer will be just another fabulous experience to add to the package? Instead, Emily starts to discover that life can be messy – and it doesn't matter how many designer clothes there are in your closet if there are skeletons lurking there too.

From Milan to London, Paris and New York, Emily does her utmost to conceal the rampant affair – Miles is her secret lover and that's the way it's going to stay. But secrets come at a cost and Emily is about to be hit with the bill. After all, you can't live on emotional credit forever . . . can you?

Subscribe to receive *read more*, your monthly newsletter from Penguin Australia. As a *read more* subscriber you'll receive sneak peeks of new books, be kept up to date with what's hot, have the opportunity to meet your favourite authors, download reading guides for your book club, receive special offers, be in the running to win exclusive subscriber-only prizes, plus much more.

Visit penguin.com.au to subscribe.